RECIPE BOOK

101 BARISTA-QUALITY ICED COFFEE & COLD BREW DRINKS YOU CAN MAKE AT HOME!

EDITION 2

BY
MIKE ALAN

HHF PRESS
SAN FRANCISCO

Legal Notice

The information contained in this book is for entertainment purposes only. The content represents the opinion of the author and is based on the author's personal experience and observations. The author does not assume any liability whatsoever for the use of or inability to use any or all information contained in this book, and accepts no responsibility for any loss or damages of any kind that may be incurred by the reader as a result of actions arising from the use of information in this book. Use this information at your own risk.

The author reserves the right to make any changes he or she deems necessary to future versions of the publication to ensure its accuracy.

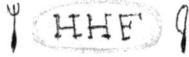

COPYRIGHT © 2016, 2020 Healthy Happy Foodie Press.

All rights reserved.

Published in the United States of America
by Healthy Happy Foodie Press.

www.HHFpress.com

Table Of Contents

Why You Need This Book!	7
Why Use the Takeya Cold Brew System	11
The Surprising Health Benefits of Cold-Brewed Coffee	16
How to Use the Takeya Cold Brew System	19
Pro Tips to Make Perfect Takeya Coffee and Other Concoctions	23
A Brief History of Coffee	26
Espresso Coffee Recipes	**30**
Almond Espresso Ice Cream Float	31
Black Russian Espresso	32
Chilled Espresso Martini	33
Espresso Royal	34
Hot Buttered Chocolate-Caramel Espresso	35
Lassi Style Espresso	36
Peppermint Espresso Cream	37
Perfect Iced Espresso	38
Sicilian Espresso Martini	39
Tangy Bourbon Espresso	40
Walnut Espresso Frappe	41
Latte Coffee Recipes	**42**
Almond Milk Cold Brew Latte	43
Amaretto Almond Latte	44
Cinnamon Dolce Latte	45

Creamy Eggnog Latte	46
Creamy Italian Coffee	47
Gingerbread Latte	48
Gingerbread Latte Supreme	49
Hot Buttered Almond Coffee	50
Hot Buttered Coffee	51
Maple Cream Latte	52
Marshmallow Cream Latte	53
Nutella Blended Latte	54
Orange Mocha Latte	55
Tembleque Latte	56
Vanilla Ginger Latte	57
White Chocolate Latte	58
Cappuccino Coffees	**59**
Authentic Cappuccino	60
Black Forest Cappuccino	61
Cinnamon Mocha Cappuccino	62
Hazelnut Cappuccino	64
Iced Eggnog Cappuccino	65
Mocha Mint Cappuccino	66
Chocolate & Caramel Coffees	**67**
Amaretto and Chocolate Coffee	68
Black Magic Chocolate Coffee	69
Brown Sugar Caramel Latte	70
Caramel Macchiato	71
Caramel Macchiato with Homemade Vanilla Syrup	72
Chocolate and Vanilla Latte	74
Mayan Coffee	75
Viennese Coffee	76
Whipped Chocolate and Vanilla Mocha	77
Mocha Coffees	**78**
Caramel Cream Mocha	79
Easy Cinnamon Mocha Latte	80
Hot Cocoa Mocha Latte	81

Mint Mocha Latte	82
Peanut Butter Mocha	83
Peppermint Mocha	84
Salted Caramel Mocha Frappuccino	85
Simple Cafe Mocha	86

Fruity and Spiced Coffees — **87**

Banana Coconut Coffee Frappe	88
Berry Mocha	89
Blueberry White Chocolate Latte	90
Chocolate-Cherry Frappe	91
Coconut Oil Coffee	92
Honey Coffee	93
Raspberry Frappe	94
Spiked Cherry Cola Cold Brew	95
Strawberry Iced Coffee	96

Iced Coffees — **97**

Blended Iced Espresso	98
Caribbean Spiced Coffee Soda	99
Chocolate-Cinnamon Iced Cappuccino	100
Coconut Mocha Iced Coffee	101
Coffee Ice Cubes	102
Cold Brewed Horchata Coffee	103
Cold Brewed Iced Mocha	104
Cold Brewed Vanilla Caramel Coffee	105
Frozen Caramel-Cinnamon Latte	106
Frozen Caramel Latte	107
Hazelnut Mocha Smoothie	108
Honey Cinnamon Iced Coffee	109
Iced Coconut Latte	110
Old Fashioned Coffee Soda	111
Simple Coffee Frappe	112
Simple Cold Brewed Coffee	113

International Coffees — **114**

African Coffee Punch	115

Authentic Irish Coffee	116
Brazilian Coffee	117
Brazilian Coffee Soda	118
Cuban Iced Coffee	119
Dublin Iced Coffee	120
Guatemalan Hop	121
Irish Cappuccino	122
Mexican Espresso	123
Spicy Thai Iced Coffee	124
Thai Coffee	126
The World's Best Pumpkin Spice Latte	127
Traditional Turkish Coffee	129
Vietnamese Coffee	130
Warm Gingerbread Irish Coffee	131

Coffee Cocktails — 132

Cafe Imperial	133
Cafe Rumba	134
Chocolate Stout Affogato	135
Coffee Liqueur	136
Creamy Cinnamon Coffee Punch	137
Creamy Spiked Coffee	138
Spiced Coffee Cocktail	139
Summer Espresso Gin Fizz	140
Sweet and Creamy Irish Coffee	141
The Dude	142
Warm Strawberry Vanilla Espresso Cocktail	143

Bonus — 144

The Perfect Takeya Tiramisu	145
Takeya Cold Brew Coffee Cheesecake	147
Takeya Cold Brew as a marinade:	154
Spice Up Sauces with Takeya Cold Brew Coffee	149

1

Why You Need This Book!

It's The Only Book Written Specifically for The Takeya Cold Brew System

Get ready to make life refreshing with delicious cold-brewed coffee from Takeya Cold Brew coffee maker. While you might find another book written on Takeya, this is the most comprehensive book written specifically for Takeya and includes everything you need to know about Takeya and more. Why is this the best book ever on Takeya? You'll find pro tips on cleaning, maintaining, and getting the most out of your delicious cold brew coffee maker. Plus, 101 scrumptious recipes to explore, with a bonus chapter that takes you beyond the brew and into even more amazing ways to use your Takeya Cold Brew coffee maker—it's not just for coffee!

Unlock Your Takeya's Potential for Amazing Coffee Creations

Not only will you learn how to turn delicious cold brew coffee into scrumptious, tantalizing iced coffee treats, you'll also get the most amazing hot coffee recipes too! The amazing coffee creations you can make, using Takeya's cold brew coffee technology, are endless. This book will inspire you to go above and beyond coffee and cream, and into a world of the delicious caramel macchiato, hot buttered almond coffee, and traditional turkish coffee brewed right in the comfort of your own home. Plus, the cold brew coffee concentrate using Takeya can be kept in the refrigerator for up to two weeks, so your coffee is super-fresh, rich, strong and conveniently located right at home.

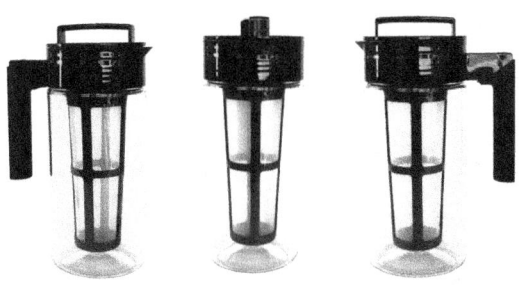

Amazing Pro Tips for Making the Best Coffee You've Ever Had

The perfect cup of coffee is right at your fingertips with the Takeya Cold Brew coffee maker. You'll learn everything you need to know and more for making the best cup of coffee you've ever had. Whether you like your coffee hot or iced, Takeya's fresh cold brew technology creates a cup of coffee that is simply out of this world. With cold brewing, only the natural, delicious coffee flavors are extracted leaving behind the bitter oils and fatty acids creating a perfectly balanced smooth extraction of concentrated coffee. It's as simple as add coffee, brew, and serve hot or iced. The best part about Takeya is that you can make, serve and store—all in one!

Over 100 Delicious Recipes for Creative Coffee Drinks

Iced coffee lovers rejoice! Hot brew coffee drinkers jump for joy! Takeya Cold Brew unites the best of both coffee worlds and gives you the ability to make coffee house and restaurant-quality coffee drinks right in the comfort of your own kitchen. The 101 delicious recipes you get with this book will inspire your creative coffee mind and take you above and beyond the perfect cup of coffee every time you brew! The best bit about this book—your Takeya Cold Brew coffee concentrate stays fresh for up to two weeks, so you don't have to make a fresh pot every night. You can enjoy delicious, tantalizing cups of creative coffee creations every morning by simply reaching into your refrigerator and turning a page to one of the amazing 101 recipes below!

It's The Only Coffee Recipe Book You'll Ever Need

Not only do you get 101 delicious recipes to experiment with, you'll also learn all the pro tips and ways to literally make the perfect cup of coffee. This book will teach you how to consistently make that perfect cup of coffee too, and maintain your Takeya Cold Brew coffee maker in order to make it time after time. Takeya's Cold Brew coffee technology allows you to quickly make the same restaurant-quality or coffee house specialty drinks that sometimes take ages. With this amazing book and Takeya Cold Brew coffee maker—you'll be able to grab your perfect cup of joe and go!

2

Why Use the Takeya Cold Brew System

The Takeya is The Absolute Best Way to Make Coffee

Takeya Cold Brew coffee maker brews possibly the best coffee you'll ever have. Why? With its amazing technology, you'll get a coffee concentrate with no bitter taste like in regular coffee makers. It makes a concentrate that tastes like freshly ground coffee beans with one very pleasant and inviting aroma, filling the kitchen air. When hot water coffee makers or drip coffee brewers are used, the bitter oils of the raw coffee bean are released right into the coffee. Even once you refrigerate the Takeya Cold Brew coffee concentrate you get a cup of coffee that tastes as good as the beans smelled when they were ground—every time.

Multiple Techniques for Creating Bold Flavors

One of the most amazing, bold reasons this book is fabulous when it comes to the Takeya Cold Brew coffee maker is you will learn multiple techniques for creating bold coffee flavors. This book is packed with pro tips on using coconut or soy milk, how to grind the coffee for the best quality cup, how to clean and maintain your cold brew coffee filter, and just how to add the perfect blend of ingredients for all those exciting specialty style brews that you thought you could only get in a restaurant or coffee house. With Takeya you'll pick up multiple techniques to make those delectable coffee drinks you crave with scrumptious Takeya Cold Brew concentrate.

The Most Convenient Way of Making Perfectly Brewed Coffee

Talk about one convenient, easy way to brew fresh coffee. When it comes to the most effortless, perfect cup of coffee, you'll love the Takeya Cold Brew coffee maker. Not only is it the most convenient way of making the most perfectly brewed coffee—it's also the easiest and most delicious way to get rich, bold, strong coffee time after time. A Turkish Proverb says, "Coffee should be black as hell, strong as death, and as sweet as love." That is exactly what you will get every time you brew with Takeya—the most convenient, perfectly brewed cup of java you've ever tasted!

The Most Durable Coffee Maker on The Market

The airtight, leak-proof lid locks in freshness and flavor. The tight seal keeps your Takeya coffee concentrate fresh for up to two weeks and helps you store pitcher horizontally, or on its side, without leaks. You get a non-slip grip with the sturdy but soft silicone handle, allowing you to move and pour coffee with ease. The pitcher itself is made from BPA-Free Tritan™ a plastic that is simply "engineered to be better." Tritan prides itself on being, "Better than glass. Better than stainless. Better than any other plastic. And Tritan doesn't contain BPA, BPS or any other bisphenols. Products made with Tritan plastic are clear, durable, safe and stylish." Not only is Takeya Cold Brew coffee maker the most durable coffee maker on the market—it's Made in the USA!

Cleaning The Takeya is Easy and Fast

Before your first use, simply wash all the components of your Takeya Cold Brew in warm soapy water. Place in a dish rack to air dry. You're ready to brew. It's that easy! After each use, remove the infuser. Turn upside down over a trash can or bin, and tap out coffee grinds. Remove excess coffee grinds by placing the infuser under the tap in the sink. Run fresh water over the infuser and tap again. Wash components in warm soapy water and air dry like above. Over time, you may want to go for a deeper clean to make the most fresh cold brew coffee possible. Simply mix a solution of 50/50 water and white vinegar. Submerge components in the solution overnight. Wash with warm soapy water and air dry. It's also dishwasher safe!

3

The Surprising Health Benefits of Cold-Brewed Coffee

Improve Your Energy and Attention

Kick start your morning and boost your energy with Takeya Cold Brew! Coffee is proven to increase focus and concentration to help you tackle the tasks at hand by helping you become more alert and mentally focused. As a stimulant, coffee can reduce fatigue and enhance short-term memory. A little coffee break now and then is also good for the mood and mind, and can help you change things up to increase achievement of your goals. Takeya Cold Brew's less acidic, smooth taste really is the perfect and super delicious way to improve your energy and attention.

Coffee Can Help You Burn Fat!

Did you know that coffee can actually boost your metabolic rate, helping you to burn calories over time? With the Takeya Cold Brew cuppa, much like the super antioxidant wielding green tea, coffee can help you burn fat! Coffee's fat-burning qualities will literally translate into big losses in calories over time. The caffeine in just one cup of Takeya Cold Brew can boost calorie burning by 4% over the course of two and half hours. So weight loss can be fun and easy—especially with over 101 delicious recipes to choose from below!

Cold Brewing Preserves Coffee's Essential Nutrients

The Takeya Cold Brew coffee maker has way more advantages to it than just smooth tastes, the technology behind cold brewing actually preserves the coffee's essential nutrients so you get all the benefits you can out of one cup. Simply because Takeya Cold Brew coffee maker eliminates a lot of the natural acidity that is normally present in traditional brewed coffee—your body is able to digest it better. That means you get all the essential nutrients and good stuff without throwing your body's ph out of whack. What you get is a simple, smooth cup of totally comforting coffee.

Can Help Prevent Diseases Such as Dementia and Parkinson's

Combat the ailments of old age with something as simple as Takeya Cold Brew coffee concentrate. According to the researchers at Medical News Today, "Researchers in the U.S. carried out a study that assessed the link between coffee consumption and Parkinson's disease risk. The authors of the study concluded that 'higher coffee and caffeine intake is associated with a significantly lower incidence of Parkinson's disease'. In addition, caffeine in coffee may help control movement in people suffering from Parkinson's, according to a study conducted at the Research Institute of the McGill University Health Centre (RI MUHC) that was published in the journal Neurology." Many similar studies have been conducted on the health benefits of coffee to conclude that drinking coffee can lower your risk of heart failure, stroke, diabetes and dementia as well.

(https://www.ncbi.nlm.nih.gov/pubmed/20182054)

Cold Brewing Unlocks Many Beneficial Antioxidants

Simply put, the heat from traditional coffee brewing not only damages the essential oils in coffee, making it taste burnt—it also damages those essential oils that are packed with beneficial antioxidants. Why? The process of heating the coffee in the coffee making process can cause a chemical reaction that morphs the coffee into a different compound altogether depleting it from its health benefits! Not only will you get a better tasting cuppa with Takeya Cold Brew, you will get a more flavorful, bold, aromatic cup too!

4
How to Use the Takeya Cold Brew System

Setting up Your Takeya in Seconds

The sweetest thing about fresh cold-brewed coffee is how easy it is to use your Takeya Cold Brew coffee maker. Before the first use, follow the quick and easy cleaning instructions above. Place the non-slip silicone handle on top of the pitcher. Next grab the premium mesh infuser, otherwise known as a filter, and place it in the pitcher. Finally, place the airtight lid on top of the Takeya and screw it on until it locks into place. You're ready for your first brew!

The Takeya is The Simplest Coffee System You've Ever Used

How simple is that!? Takeya really is the simplest coffee system you've ever used. With quick assembly time also comes quick cleaning and maintaining time too! A good pro tip for before brewing is to check the "O" ring seal in the airtight lid is properly placed on the lid and in between the handle assemble and the body of the Takeya Cold Brew coffee maker to prevent leakage. That's one simple coffee system when it all comes down to making a smooth cup of joe.

How to Use Steeping Times to Your Advantage

To make your perfect cup of coffee using your Takeya Cold Brew, you'll want to take advantage of testing out steeping times to get it just right. For those who like a mild yet robust cup of bright morning "joe", you'll want to steep for 12 hours. For the coffee drinker that likes coffee a little more on the dark side with a smooth, rich flavor— go for a 24-hour steep. And for the coffee lover who likes their coffee more along the Italian espresso style side, you will want to try a 48-hour steep. The flavor of coffee changes with time, so coffee lovers will find it fun to experiment with brew times to find their perfectly balanced brew.

Use The Takeya to Make Amazing Iced or Hot Coffee

The most amazing part about the Takeya Cold Brew coffee maker is that you can enjoy both iced and hot coffee! For iced coffee lovers, just remove the Takeya coffee concentrate from the refrigerator. Fill a glass with ice, pour coffee concentrate into a glass, top with milk or cream and mix in the sweetener of your choice. Mix one-part coffee concentrate with two parts boiling water and stir in cream and sweetener if desired.

How to Make Concentrated Cold Brew Coffee with The Takeya

Once you've cleaned and assembled your Takeya Cold Brew coffee maker, simply add coffee to your premium mesh infuser. Depending on your desired strength, add 14 to 16 tablespoons of your favorite medium or dark roast, coarsely ground coffee to the infuser. Twist the infuser into the airtight lid. Add four cups of cold, filtered water to the Takeya pitcher. Lower the infuser into the water, seal the lid airtight to lock in freshness and place the Takeya Cold Brew coffee maker into the refrigerator for 12 to 48 hours. During brewing, remove the Takeya pitcher and open and swirl the infuser on occasion.

How to Brew Coffee Using the Takeya

STEP 1:

Add water to the Takeya pitcher and spoon coffee into the infuser.

STEP 2:

Twist and seal lid into the pitcher airtight.

STEP 3:

Shake well and place in refrigerator for 12-48 hours, depending on your preference. Note: Refrigerate longer for coffee concentrate.

5

Pro Tips to Make Perfect Takeya Coffee and Other Concoctions

Make Coffee That is The Perfect Strength for You

A lot of coffee strength comes down to grind and type of coffee used. A medium ground coffee will have a sweetness that stays with you, while a coarse ground coffee brewed in the Takeya will have a dark sweetness that leaves the palate quickly. When you experiment with strength, try using various types of coffee and grinds. A light morning blend will yield a less strong cup of joe, while a dark coffee tends to give cold brew drinkers a more donut-shoppe-quality cup of coffee. No matter what, you can't go wrong with the 101 scrumptious recipes below. You'll have so much fun experimenting with Takeya, you'll never make a hot brewed cup again.

Make Coffee with Less Acid for a Smoother Flavor

Takeya Cold-brewed coffee is simply so smooth you might not believe it until you try it! Because the cold brew process creates a less acidic coffee, you don't get the "burnt toast" taste some hot brewed coffees give off. It literally creates a smoother flavor when you brew the coffee using the cold brew technology. This is all due to the fact that cold brewing coffee doesn't chemically alter essential oils of the coffee bean. The reduced acid also has massive health benefits! It's not only healthier for your teeth, but your sensitive stomach too. So you get less acid smoother flavor and digestive qualities with Takeya Cold Brew coffee maker.

Spice Up Your Daily Coffee with Exotic Flavors

Take your taste buds on a total taste adventure with exotic flavors from all over the world. If you love to spice things up and try new recipes, the 101 ways below will have you going on a world expedition right in the comfort of your own kitchen. From Turkish delights to African coffee punch and a Guatemalan hop—get ready to heat things up at home! You might enjoy your daily coffee with cream and sugar, but after you explore the delicious recipes below you'll be ready to spice up your daily coffee with sensual, sweet and spicy exotic flavors galore.

The Right Amount of Water Makes all The Difference

When it comes to brewing the perfect cup of Takeya Cold Brew coffee, the right amount of water makes all the difference. Four cups. That's it. No more. No less. You'll want to use filtered water too! Since the KIND of water also makes a massive difference! If you've ever experienced sediment or build up in a traditional coffee maker, it all comes down to using water out of a tap that can become calcified depending on what the local water plant uses to treat the water in order to make it drinkable. Filtered or bottled water has the best taste and is sediment-free, so your Takeya Cold Brew coffee is perfect to the last drop!

The Best Way to Store Your Cold-Brewed Coffee

Best way to store you cold brew: in the refrigerator. That's it. Simply keep it cold for up to two weeks and you've got convenient, fresh coffee right at your fingertips. The cool thing about the Takeya Cold Brew coffee maker is that the airtight lid prevents spilling—so you can make room for it in the fridge by keeping it upright or on its side.

6

A Brief History of Coffee

The Origins of Coffee

Some coffee historians claim the origins of coffee are virtually unknown, that the origin of coffee comes from various legends from all over the world. It seemed for a while that everyone had their own stake in the origin of the beautiful bean. Most historians believe coffee originated in Ethiopia from a "magical fruit" with a white blossom that smelled like jasmine. From Yemen to Istanbul, Venice to Vienna, Paris to London, the rumor of this concoction with its medicinal properties spread to lands far and beyond for years and years. The plant was first discovered in Ethiopia in the 11th Century giving it the claim to coffee and all its glorious fame.

Coffees of The World: The Difference Between Regions

Coffee today comes from all over the world with vastly different tastes, textures, and aromas. Some love a good Colombian brew, while others enjoy the aromatic brew of a Kona bean. What's the difference in regions? Each kind of coffee simply has different taste and aromas due to the difference in the atmosphere in which it is grown. Coffee from the Hawaiian region of Kona is rich and aromatic with a medium body due to the volcanic soil that it is grown in. Mexican coffee is grown in high altitudes, so it tends to have sharp flavor with lots of depth. Costa Rican coffee is grown in small farms then wet processed giving it what most people refer to as "perfect balance". Want a delicate, mild bodied coffee with an aromatic sweetness—then you'll love the care, attention and pride that is given to growing coffee in rugged Columbia on small, family farms. Want a full-bodied, bold, full-flavor coffee? Then look no further than the birthplace of coffee, the coffee tree forests of Ethiopia are the perfect place for a genuinely bold cup of joe.

Regular Coffee vs. Espresso

Quite often some people believe the difference between regular coffee and espresso comes down to taste. Sometimes they think it's all about the level of grind. You might see a bag of coffee beans or ground coffee labeled espresso, but it's not actually the type of roast or the grind at all. It's the brewing process! Espresso is made by forcing steam into the ground coffee. Regular coffee is made by pouring water over ground beans in a filter. They also taste different. Because regular coffee is coarse, it tends to be very robust and bright. While Espresso is black as night, dark as hell; the bean is very finely ground, almost like a powder, and extremely aromatic. Nevertheless, the difference between Regular Coffee and Espresso all comes down to how it's brewed.

Choosing The Right Roast for Your Daily Coffee

The goal in roasting is to bring out the best quality in the coffee beans for a perfectly smooth, balanced cup of coffee, no matter what you like when it comes to your daily cup. Some people enjoy a light, bright roast. Some a medium and rich cup of joe. Then there are those that like a darker roast bean full of aroma. If you like a light roast coffee, you'll want to go for beans that are labeled: Morning Blend, Light, Kenya AA, Peaberry, Colombian, and Guatemalan. For those that like a medium roast coffee look for labels with American, Breakfast, Medium, Ethiopia and Costa Rica. If you are looking for a dark roast coffee try French, Italian, Espresso, Dark, Viennese, Sumatra or Mocha Java.

The Takeya Works with All Types of Coffee

The most amazing part about the Takeya Cold Brew Coffee Maker is that no matter what roast you like, how dark or light you like your coffee to taste, how coarsely or fine you normally grind your favorite coffee beans: The Takeya Cold Brew Coffee Maker works with ALL types of coffee. Simply grind up your favorite beans, mix and match the beans you buy for your own unique coffee blend, or buy your favorite bean already ground. No matter what you brew up using your Takeya—you are going to love experimenting with this amazing cold brew coffee maker.

7

Espresso Coffee Recipes

Almond Espresso Ice Cream Float

*Servings: 4 | Prep Time: 20 minutes |
Cook Time: 24 - 48 hours*

Delicious on a hot day or as an after dinner treat, you can turn your cold brew into tantalizing desserts! The Almond Espresso Ice Cream Float is simply perfect any time you crave a sweet coffee treat.

Ingredients:

14-16 tablespoons "natural processed" dark roast coffee, coarsely ground
1 quart cold, filtered water
2 cups cold milk
4 tablespoons chocolate syrup
1/8 teaspoon almond extract or 1 tablespoon almond syrup
4 scoops coffee or espresso ice cream
2 cans cream soda
Whipped cream, for topping

Instructions:

1. Add water and almond extract to the Takeya pitcher and spoon coffee into the infuser.
2. Brew coffee (page 22).
3. Chill two tall glasses in the freezer and when they are cold, add one scoop of ice cream to each glass.
4. Pour the coffee into the milk; then pour the coffee over the ice cream.
5. Fill each glass with the cream soda and top each glass with one tablespoon of chocolate syrup.
6. Top with whipped cream and serve!

Black Russian Espresso

*Servings: 4 | Prep Time: 25 minutes |
Cook Time: 12 - 24 hours*

Mix up a decadent espresso cocktail that combines the rich strong flavor of Takeya Cold Brew coffee with a traditional Black Russian cocktail for one sincerely elegant after dinner drink.

Ingredients:
14-16 tablespoons "natural processed" dark roast coffee, coarsely ground
1 quart cold, filtered water
4 ounces kahlua coffee liqueur
4 ounces vodka
Ice cubes

Instructions:
1. Brew coffee in Takeya pitcher (page 22).
2. Combine 1/2 a pitcher of cold brew espresso, Kahlua, vodka, and ice in a shaker. Shake well.
3. Strain into chilled martini glasses and serve.

Chilled Espresso Martini

*Servings: 4 | Prep Time: 25 minutes |
Cook Time: 12 - 24 hours*

Chill your favorite cold brew for one timeless cocktail. This elegant coffee cocktail is sure to be a hit at your next part, or whip up a batch any time and enjoy one classy espresso drink.

Ingredients:
14-16 tablespoons "natural processed" dark roast coffee, coarsely ground
1 quart cold, filtered water
4 ounces vodka
3 ounces crème de cacao
3 ounces Kahlua
Ice cubes

Instructions:
1. Brew coffee in Takeya pitcher (page 22).
2. Combine the coffee, vodka, Kahlua, and crème de cacao, and ice in a cocktail shaker. Shake well and pour into chilled martini glasses.

Espresso Royal

Servings: 4 | Prep Time: 20 minutes | Cook Time: 24 - 48 hours

A sophisticated after dinner coffee that combines Cognac with the rich flavor of cold brew coffee, you'll love this Takeya inspired recipe. The Espresso Royal will give you one fabulous reason to throw a dinner party.

Ingredients:

14-16 tablespoons "natural processed" dark roast coffee, coarsely ground
1 quart cold, filtered water
4 parts boiling water
4 ounces cognac or brandy
2 tablespoons sugar
1 cup heavy cream

Instructions:

1. Brew coffee in Takeya pitcher (page 22).
2. Place a metal mixing bowl and metal whisk into the freezer for 10 to 15 minutes.
3. Whip the heavy cream and sugar in the large metal mixing bowl so that it is very stiff.
4. Divide the coffee into four mugs and top with one part boiling water. Add one ounce of cognac each.
5. Top with whipped cream and serve immediately.

Hot Buttered Chocolate-Caramel Espresso

*Servings: 4 | Prep Time: 5 minutes |
Cook Time: 24 hours*

When decadently smooth butter meets dark roasted coffee, chocolate and caramel—get ready for one seriously amazing dessert coffee. Perfect as an after dinner treat or afternoon snack, this coffee always hits the sweet spot.

Ingredients:
*14-16 tablespoons "natural processed" dark roast coffee,
coarsely ground
1 quart cold, filtered water
4 teaspoons brown sugar
4 teaspoons butter
4 tablespoons chocolate syrup
8 ounces spiced rum, like Captain
Morgan or Sailor Jerry
4 parts boiling water*

Instructions:
1. Brew coffee in Takeya pitcher (page 22).
2. Divide the coffee between four mugs. Combine the sugar, butter, and chocolate syrup in a small mixing bowl; whisk until well-blended.
3. Divide the coffee into four mugs and top with one part boiling water.
4. Stir 1/4 of the butter and sugar mix into each mug until dissolved.
5. Slowly pour 2 ounces of rum into each coffee and serve!

Lassi Style Espresso

*Servings: 4 | Prep Time: 5 minutes |
Cook Time: 12 - 24 hours*

Brew up one Middle Eastern inspired coffee treat. Rich and smooth, thanks to the addition of yogurt, this creamy and cool drink is sure to warm your soul any time of the day.

Ingredients:
14-16 tablespoons "natural processed" dark roast coffee, coarsely ground
1 quart cold, filtered water
2 cups vanilla flavored yogurt
1 cup half and half or milk
4 tablespoons sugar
Ice cubes

Instructions:
1. Brew coffee in Takeya pitcher (page 22).
2. Fill two glasses with ice and spoon in a half cup of yogurt into each.
3. Add 1/4 cup half and half, and 1 tablespoon of sugar to each glass.
4. Pour half of the espresso into each glass, stir well and serve.

Peppermint Espresso Cream

*Servings: 4 | Prep Time: 5 minutes |
Cook Time: 12 - 24 hours*

Let your Takeya Cold Brew Coffee shine bright with a pop of peppermint in your favorite style espresso brew. Creamy and decadent this drink is the perfect after dinner treat to cleanse your palette.

Ingredients:
14-16 tablespoons coffee, coarsely ground
1 quart cold, filtered water
2 teaspoons peppermint extract
8 tablespoons heavy cream or half and half
Sugar or sugar substitute (optional)

Instructions:
1. Brew coffee in Takeya pitcher (page 22).
2. Divide the coffee between four mugs.
3. Top each with one part boiling water.
   Add 1/2 teaspoon of the peppermint extract to each cup.
4. Stir two tablespoons of heavy cream into each cup.
5. Sweeten if desired and serve.

Perfect Iced Espresso

*Servings: 4 | Prep Time: 5 minutes |
Cook Time: 24 - 48 hours*

If you love the velvety complex, rich flavors of espresso this is the recipe for you. Coffee house style iced espresso is right at your fingertips with the Takeya Cold Brew Coffee Maker.

Ingredients:
14-16 tablespoons "natural processed" dark roast coffee, coarsely ground
1 quart cold, filtered water
Ice
4 tablespoons half and half (optional)
4 teaspoon sugar or sugar substitute (optional)

Instructions:
1. Brew coffee in Takeya pitcher (page 22).
2. Add ice to four glasses and pour the cold brew espresso over the ice and add one tablespoon of half and half and/or sugar to each glass. Serve immediately and enjoy.

Sicilian Espresso Martini

*Servings: 4 | Prep Time: 25 Minutes |
Cook Time: 12 - 24 hours*

Turn your Takeya Cold Brew Coffee Maker into cocktail hour. This sophisticated coffee martini hybrid is the perfect cocktail for happy hour at home or as an after dinner drink.

Ingredients:
14-16 tablespoons coffee, coarsely ground
1 quart cold, filtered water
1 ounce sweet vermouth
4 ounces Aperol
4 ounces sparkling water
Ice cubes
Orange slices, for garnish

Instructions:
1. Brew coffee in Takeya pitcher (page 22).
2. In a cocktail shaker, combine a half pitcher of coffee, vermouth, Aperol, and ice. Shake well.
3. Pour into four chilled martini glasses.
4. Top with one ounce of sparkling water and garnish with a slice of orange.

Tangy Bourbon Espresso

*Servings: 4 | Prep Time: 10 minutes |
Cook Time: 12 - 24 hours*

A truly complex espresso that combines citrus, spices, and bourbon for full robust flavors and lots of subtle undertones. This tangy drink is perfect for relaxing on a cold evening or for entertaining friends and family.

Ingredients:
14-16 tablespoons "natural processed" dark roast coffee, coarsely ground
1 quart cold, filtered water
4 parts boiling water
Zest of 1 orange
1 teaspoon ground cinnamon
1 teaspoon ground cardamom
1/2 teaspoon ground cloves
4 tablespoons sugar
4 tablespoons half and half
4 ounces bourbon

Instructions:
1. Brew coffee in Takeya pitcher (page 22).
2. Divide the cold brew espresso into four mugs and top each with one part boiling water.
3. Add one tablespoon of sugar, one ounce of bourbon and one tablespoon of half and half to each mug. Stir until the sugar is dissolved and serve.

Walnut Espresso Frappe

*Servings: 4 | Prep Time: 10 minutes |
Cook Time: 12 - 24 hours*

Kick things up a notch after dinner with this delicious nutty dessert coffee. With just the right blend of flavors, thanks to earthy walnuts and natural vanilla, you'll fall in love with this drink and make it your new fall or winter favorite!

Ingredients:
14-16 tablespoons coffee, coarsely ground
1 quart cold, filtered water
1 cup walnuts
4 tablespoon chocolate syrup
4 scoops vanilla ice cream
2 cups cold, ultra-filtered milk
2 teaspoons vanilla extract
Whipped cream (optional)

Instructions:
1. Brew coffee in Takeya pitcher (page 22).
2. Add the walnuts, chocolate syrup, milk, ice cream, vanilla extract, and coffee to a blender; pulse until well-blended.
3. Divide the coffee between four chilled glasses. Top with whipped cream, if desired. Serve with straw.

8

Latte Coffee Recipes

Almond Milk Cold Brew Latte

*Servings: 4 | Prep Time: 2 hours and 20 minutes |
Cook Time: 12 - 24 hours*

Simple, flavorful and fun, this drink slowly releases the taste of robust coffee into delicious almond milk. One sincerely creative latte, you decide how much coffee flavor you like or how little you'd like to savor.

Ingredients:
14-16 tablespoons coffee, coarsely ground
1 quart cold, filtered water
4 cups almond milk
Sugar or sugar substitute (optional)

Instructions:
1. Brew coffee in Takeya pitcher (page 22).
2. Pour coffee into ice cube trays and place in the freezer for two hours. Once frozen, divide them into four glasses.
3. Pour 1 cup of the almond milk over the coffee cubes and stir.
4. Sweeten to taste, if desired and serve.
   As the cubes melt they will continue to add more and more flavor to the almond milk.

Amaretto Almond Latte

*Servings: 4 | Prep Time: 10 minutes |
Cook Time: 12 - 24 hours*

This Italian inspired after dinner coffee is the perfect finish to any meal. Bring out the bold flavor of your Takeya coffee with toasted almonds and sweet amaretto.

Ingredients:

14-16 tablespoons coffee, coarsely ground
1 quart cold, filtered water
4 ounces Amaretto liqueur
1 tablespoon almond extract
2 cups steamed milk
Whipped cream (optional)

Instructions:

1. Brew coffee in Takeya pitcher (page 22).
2. In a pitcher, combine the coffee, Amaretto, and almond extract.
3. Heat milk in a microwave on high for 30 seconds to 1 minute, or until steam begins to rise on the milk.
4. Stir the steamed milk into the pitcher with the coffee. Serve with whipped cream if desired.

Cinnamon Dolce Latte

*Servings: 4 | Prep Time: 5 minutes |
Cook Time: 24 hours*

Spice up your regular latte with a little spice and a lot of bold sweetness. Cinnamon Dolce Latte is filled with creamy sweet textures that remind you of Italy. Add a little whipped cream and it becomes a delicious dessert coffee!

Ingredients:
*14-16 tablespoons "natural processed" dark roast
Coffee, coarsely ground
1 quart cold, filtered water
2 cups frothed milk
2 tablespoons cinnamon syrup
Whipped cream, for topping (optional)
Cinnamon and sugar, for topping (optional)*

Instructions:
1. Brew coffee in Takeya pitcher (page 22).
2. Pour milk into a microwave safe dish. Heat in a microwave on high for 30 seconds to 1 minute, or until steam begins to rise on the milk.
3. Fold the cinnamon syrup into the frothed milk.
4. Divide the coffee between four mugs.
5. Top coffee with a 1/2 cup of the cinnamon latte.
6. Top with whipped cream and sprinkle with cinnamon sugar.
7. Tip: For a relaxing after dinner coffee, try adding one ounce of cognac or brandy.

Creamy Eggnog Latte

Servings: 4 | Prep Time: 5 minutes | Cook Time: 12 - 24 hours

Whip up a mug of a treasured classic holiday drink. The Creamy Eggnog Latte is full of sweet spice and creamy nog sure to spice up any holiday party or an evening by the fire.

Ingredients:

14-16 tablespoons "natural processed" dark roast coffee, coarsely ground
1 quart cold, filtered water
2 cups eggnog
2 cups frothed milk
2 ounces kentucky bourbon, like Maker's Mark (optional)
Cinnamon sticks or cinnamon sugar, for garnish

Instructions:

1. Brew coffee in Takeya pitcher (page 22).
2. Pour milk into a microwave safe dish. Heat in a microwave on high for 30 seconds to 1 minute, or until steam begins to rise on the milk.
3. Divide the coffee between four mugs. Add one 1/2 cup of the eggnog and milk to each mug.
4. Slowly add 2 ounces of bourbon per mug if desired; stirring well.
5. Garnish with cinnamon to serve.
6. You can also omit the frothed milk and serve this over ice for one killer iced coffee or holiday cocktail!

Creamy Italian Coffee

*Servings: 4 | Prep Time: 5 minutes |
Cook Time: 12 - 24 hours*

Add some sweet Italian spice to your morning cup of joe! This delicious coffee can be served both hot or cold for a tantalizing way to wake up in the morning.

Ingredients:
14-16 tablespoons coffee, coarsely ground
1 quart cold, filtered water
2 cinnamon sticks, broken in half
1 whole nutmeg, crushed
2 cups frothed milk
4 teaspoons sugar or sugar substitute (optional)

Instructions:
1. Add water to the Takeya pitcher and spoon coffee into the infuser.
2. Push cinnamon sticks and nutmeg into the coffee.
3. Brew coffee in Takeya pitcher (page 22).
4. Divide the coffee between four mugs.
5. Pour milk into a microwave safe dish.
6. Heat in a microwave on high for 30 seconds to 1 minute, or until steam begins to rise on the milk.
7. Add half of the frothed milk to each mug.
8. Add sugar if desired. Serve immediately.

Gingerbread Latte

*Servings: 4 | Prep Time: 10 minutes |
Cook Time: 12 - 24 hours*

Perfect for entertaining around the holidays, this delicious latte is full of sweet spice. You'll love brewing up this specialty with your Takeya Cold Brew Maker so much—that you just might invite friends and family over to share a little joy with you.

Ingredients:

14-16 tablespoons coffee, coarsely ground
1 quart cold, filtered water
2 cups steamed milk
1 tablespoon sugar
1 tablespoon gingerbread spice or allspice
Whipped cream (optional)

Instructions:

1. Mix coffee and gingerbread spice in a small mixing bowl and spoon coffee into the infuser.
2. Brew coffee in Takeya pitcher (page 22).
3. Divide coffee between four mugs. Add 1/2 cup of steamed milk to each mug.
4. Add the sugar and stir. Serve with whipped cream, if desired.

Gingerbread Latte Supreme

*Servings: 4 | Prep Time: 20 minutes |
Cook Time: 12 - 24 hours*

This full flavored coffee drink combines warm spices for one complex and delicious coffee drink that will awaken the senses and satisfy any taste buds. Perfect for a brisk autumn day!

Ingredients:
14-16 tablespoons coffee, coarsely ground
1 quart cold, filtered water
1/4 cup molasses
1/4 cup brown sugar
1 teaspoon ground ginger
1 teaspoon ground cinnamon
1 cup milk, frothed
1 teaspoon ground cloves
Whipped cream, for topping

Instructions:
1. Brew coffee in Takeya pitcher (page 22).
2. Combine the molasses, brown sugar, ginger, ground cloves and cinnamon in a small bowl; mix well and place in the refrigerator for 20 minutes.
3. Pour milk into a microwave safe dish. Heat in a microwave on high for 30 seconds to 1 minute, or until steam begins to rise on the milk.
4. Grab four coffee mugs and add a tablespoon of the spice blend to each mug. Top with frothed milk and stir until spice blend is dissolved. Divide the coffee amongst the four mugs, top with whipped cream and serve.

Hot Buttered Almond Coffee

*Servings: 4 | Prep Time: 5 minutes |
Cook Time: 12 hours*

Give your hot buttered coffee a little twist with almond for a rich coffee drink that will remind you of sweet almond torte! A light refreshing drink, you'll want to serve this all day long or as a complement to any dessert at a dinner party.

Ingredients:

14-16 tablespoons coffee, coarsely ground
1 quart cold, filtered water
2 teaspoons almond extract
4 teaspoons grass-fed butter
4 parts boiling water
2 teaspoon honey

Instructions:

1. Brew coffee in Takeya pitcher (page 22).
2. Divide the coffee evenly between four coffee mugs.
3. Add 1 part boiling water to each and stir.
4. Fold 1 teaspoon of butter and 1/2 teaspoon of honey per mug.
5. Stir until well-blended and enjoy it while it's hot.

Hot Buttered Coffee

*Servings: 4 | Prep Time: 5 minutes |
Cook Time: 24 hours*

Want to ramp up your morning routine with some super smooth sustained energy? You'll love the benefits from this hip trend also known as Bulletproof Coffee.

Ingredients
14-16 tablespoons coffee, coarsely ground
1 quart cold, filtered water
4 tablespoons unsalted grass-fed butter, like Kerrygold
4 parts boiling water

Instructions:
1. Brew coffee in Takeya pitcher (page 22).
2. Divide the coffee into four mugs; add one part boiling water to each mug.
3. Stir 1 tablespoon of butter into each mug and enjoy.
4. To make your buttered coffee even more rich, try adding a teaspoon of sugar.
5. Pour the coffee into a blender, or use a hand frothier to whip the coffee while adding the butter and sugar; when coffee is nicely whipped, return it to the original mug and enjoy.

Maple Cream Latte

*Servings: 4 | Prep Time: 10 minutes |
Cook Time: 5 minutes*

The flavor of pure maple syrup is infused in the milk for this rich and creamy latte that embodies the feelings of a brisk fall day in New England. For best results use real A-grade maple syrup.

Ingredients:
14-16 tablespoons coffee, coarsely ground
1 quart cold, filtered water
1/4 cup pure maple syrup
1 cup whole milk
Whipped cream (optional)

Instructions:
1. Brew coffee in Takeya pitcher (page 22).
2. Divide the coffee between four mugs.
3. Heat the milk in a small sauce pan on medium heat.
4. Add the maple syrup and turn stove to low heat; stir well until all of the maple syrup has dissolved into the milk and steam begins to rise.
5. Divide the hot maple latte between the 4 mugs. Then top with whipped cream.

Marshmallow Cream Latte

*Servings: 4 | Prep Time: 5 minutes |
Cook Time: 12 - 24 hours*

If you like your coffee sweet, you'll fall in love with this latte. Add a little light and airy marshmallow to your cold brew coffee and you've got one seriously decadent dessert drink.

Ingredients:
14-16 tablespoons coffee, coarsely ground
1 quart cold, filtered water
2/3 cups marshmallow fluff
1 1/2 cups frothed milk
Whipped cream (optional)

Instructions:
1. Brew coffee in Takeya pitcher (page 22).
2. Pour milk into a microwave safe dish. Heat in a microwave on high for 30 seconds to 1 minute, or until steam begins to rise on the milk.
3. Fold the marshmallow fluff into the frothed milk; whisk until well dissolved.
4. Divide the milk mixture between the 4 coffee mugs and stir well. Top with whipped cream, if desired.

Nutella Blended Latte

Servings: 4 | Prep Time: 20 minutes | Cook Time: 5 minutes

When hazelnut meets chocolate, you get one creamy sweet Italian inspired treat. This is the kind of coffee to whip up for a relaxing night in or an easy Sunday morning.

Ingredients:
14-16 tablespoons "natural processed" dark roast coffee, coarsely ground
1 quart cold, filtered water
3 cups cold milk
2 teaspoons pure vanilla extract
1/4 cup nutella
2 1/2 cups ice
Whipped cream (optional)

Instructions:
1. Brew coffee in Takeya pitcher (page 22).
2. In a blender, combine the coffee, milk, vanilla extract, Nutella, and ice. Blend well.
3. Divide the drink amongst four tall glasses. Top with whipped cream if desired and serve.

Orange Mocha Latte

*Servings: 4 | Prep Time: 10 minutes |
Cook Time: 12 - 24 hours*

Enjoy the taste of Christmas all year around with this fruity take on the traditional mocha latte. This sweet drink combines the flavor of orange zest with robust espresso and dark chocolate to create one uniquely bright and complex drink.

Ingredients:

14-16 tablespoons "natural processed" dark roast coffee, coarsely ground
1 quart cold, filtered water
1 cup hot milk
4 tablespoons dark chocolate sauce
1 tablespoon sugar or sugar substitute

For Orange Zest:

1 tablespoon orange zest
1 square of cheesecloth

Instructions:

1. Brew coffee in Takeya pitcher (page 22).
2. Lay orange zest into the middle of a square of cheesecloth. Gather the edges and tie together with string.
3. Heat the milk, sugar, and orange zest bag on medium heat until it becomes frothy. Remove from heat. Remove orange zest bag.
4. Fold dark chocolate sauce into milk until well-blended.
5. Divide the coffee into four mugs and pour 1/4 of the orange chocolate milk into each mug and serve.

Tembleque Latte

*Servings: 4 | Prep Time: 5 minutes |
Cook Time: 12 - 24 hours*

Turn your Takeya cold brew coffee into a Puerto Rican delicacy. This coconut infused latte can be served hot or cold, depending on your mood. No matter which way you choose to serve it, you'll love this rich and flavorful drink.

Ingredients:

14-16 tablespoons coffee, coarsely ground
1 quart cold, filtered water
1 cup warm milk
4 ounces coconut cream
2 teaspoons sugar or sugar substitute
Ground cinnamon, for topping

Instructions:

1. Brew coffee in Takeya pitcher (page 22).
2. Divide the coffee between 4 mugs.
3. Pour milk into a microwave safe dish and heat in a microwave on high until steam begins to rise on the milk.
4. Whisk the coconut cream and sugar into the milk until well-blended.
5. Divide the coconut milk between the 4 mugs. Stir well. Dust with cinnamon.

Vanilla Ginger Latte

*Servings: 4 | Prep Time: 5 minutes |
Cook Time: 24 hours*

Spicy ginger meets creamy vanilla for one hot little treat. Fresh ginger infused in coffee is the perfect cup of joe to keep your immune system healthy in winter months, plus this drink is sure to send your taste buds soaring. So drink up!

Ingredients:
14-16 tablespoons coffee, coarsely ground
1 quart cold, filtered water
2 teaspoons fresh sliced ginger
1 teaspoon pure vanilla extract
2 cups half and half, frothed

Instructions:
1. Add water and vanilla extract to the Takeya pitcher.
2. Brew coffee in Takeya pitcher (page 22).
3. Divide the coffee between 4 coffee mugs.
4. Pour the half and half into a microwave safe dish. Heat in a microwave on high until steam begins to rise on the half and half.
5. Stir 1/4 of the frothed half and half into each mug. Serve immediately and enjoy.

White Chocolate Latte

*Servings: 4 | Prep Time: 10 minutes |
Cook Time: 12 - 24 hours*

This sweet treat is great after a nice meal or first thing in the morning. And since the Takeya offers such flavorful cold brew coffee it will complement the sweet and creamy white chocolate like a charm.

Ingredients:
14-16 tablespoons coffee, coarsely ground
1 quart cold, filtered water
2 cups hot milk
1/2 teaspoon vanilla extract
1/2 cup white chocolate chips
Whipped cream (optional)

Instructions:
1. Brew coffee in Takeya pitcher (page 22).
2. Heat the milk in a large saucepan on medium heat, and add the white chocolate. Stir until the chocolate and milk have combined very well.
3. Stir the coffee into the milk mixture and divide into 4 mugs. Top with whipped cream, if desired.

9

Cappuccino Coffees

Authentic Cappuccino

*Servings: 4 | Prep Time: 10 minutes |
Cook Time: 24 - 48 hours*

Italian bar inspired coffee is perfect served with your favorite donut or biscotti. This coffee drink is simple and easy to make. Turn your morning into something super sweet with this tantalizing drink.

Ingredients:

14-16 tablespoons "natural processed" dark roast coffee, coarsely ground
1 quart cold, filtered water
2 cups frothed milk
Cocoa powder, for dusting
Sugar or sugar substitute, for serving

Instructions:

1. Brew coffee in Takeya pitcher (page 22).
2. Divide the coffee between 4 mugs.
   Heat the milk in a small saucepan on medium heat until frothy and nearly boiling.
3. Divide milk between the four mugs and dust each with cocoa powder.
4. Sweeten to taste, if desired, and enjoy piping hot!

Black Forest Cappuccino

*Servings: 4 | Prep Time: 10 minutes |
Cook Time: 12 - 24 hours*

The sweet combination of espresso, dark chocolate, and cherries gives this drink it's unique appeal. Serve up a special after dinner version of this coffee drink and add an ounce of brandy or cognac.

Ingredients:
14-16 tablespoons "natural processed" dark roast coffee, coarsely ground
1 quart cold, filtered water
4 ounces dark chocolate syrup
4 ounces cherry syrup or cherry puree
1 1/2 cups frothed milk
Ground cinnamon, for topping

Instructions:
1. Brew coffee in Takeya pitcher (page 22).
2. Heat the milk in a small saucepan on medium heat. Stir in the dark chocolate and cherry syrup until the flavors are well combined with the milk.
3. Divide the milk mixture between the four coffee mugs.
4. Spoon some milk foam on top of each cup and garnish with ground cinnamon.

Cinnamon Mocha Cappuccino

*Servings: 4 | Prep Time: 10 minutes |
Cook Time: 24 hours minutes*

Spice up your morning cuppa joe when cinnamon meets cocoa. Cinnamon Mocha Cappuccino is the perfect drink for sweater weather.

Ingredients:

14-16 tablespoons coffee, coarsely ground
1 quart cold, filtered water
2 cinnamon sticks
1 cup milk, frothed
1 teaspoon ground cinnamon, for topping
2 tablespoons cocoa powder
1 teaspoon sugar or sugar substitute, per mug

Instructions:

1. Add water to Takeya pitcher and spoon coffee into the infuser.
2. Break cinnamon sticks in half and shove into the coffee infuser with ground coffee.
3. Brew coffee in Takeya pitcher (page 22).
4. Pour the milk into a microwave safe bowl and microwave on high for about 1 1/2 minutes, or until steam rises off the milk, so that the milk is hot but not quite boiling. (This can also be done on the stove in a sauce pan.)
5. Whisk cocoa powder into the hot frothy milk until well-blended.
6. Divide the coffee into four mugs; add one part boiling water to each.
Add sugar to coffee if desired.

7. Stir 1/4 of the frothed chocolate milk into each mug.
8. Sprinkle each with ground cinnamon and serve.

Hazelnut Cappuccino

*Servings: 4 | Prep Time: 10 minutes |
Cook Time: 12 - 24 hours*

Nutty hazelnut with robust coffee is one supremely decadent drink. Serve on a cold winter night or as an after dinner treat with Italian liqueur for an extra decadent dessert.

Ingredients:

14-16 tablespoons "natural processed" dark roast coffee, coarsely ground

1 quart cold, filtered water

4 ounces hazelnut syrup

1 1/2 cup frothed milk

2 teaspoons sugar

Whipped cream, for topping

Ground cinnamon, for topping

Instructions:

1. Brew coffee in Takeya pitcher (page 22).
2. Heat the milk in a small saucepan on medium heat, and whisk until it begins to froth.
3. Add the hazelnut syrup and sugar to the milk and whisk until dissolved.
4. Divide the milk between 4 coffee mugs. Top whipped cream and cinnamon.

Iced Eggnog Cappuccino

*Servings: 4 | Prep Time: 20 minutes |
Cook Time: 12 - 24 hours*

We've already covered the classic eggnog latte, but this twist on a holiday favorite is great any time you're looking for a rich and playful coffee drink. Spice things up any time of year with this creamy sweet treat!

Ingredients:
14-16 tablespoons coffee, coarsely ground
1 quart cold, filtered water
1 cup cold milk
1 cup eggnog
1 teaspoon vanilla extract
1/2 teaspoon ground cinnamon
1/2 teaspoon all spice
Ice cubes

Instructions:
1. Brew coffee in Takeya pitcher (page 22).
2. Combine the milk, eggnog, vanilla extract, ground cinnamon in a large mixing bowl and whisk until well-blended.
3. Fill 4 glasses with ice and divide the coffee between each.
4. Top each with 1/4 of the eggnog mix.
   Stir each glass well and serve with a straw.

Mocha Mint Cappuccino

Servings: 4 | Prep Time: 5 minutes | Cook Time: 5 minutes

Kick things up a notch with this creamy, cool cappuccino drink. With rich, decadent chocolate and a fresh hint of mint this espresso drink is sure to liven up your morning or afternoon.

Ingredients:

14-16 tablespoons "natural processed" dark roast coffee, coarsely ground
1 quart cold, filtered water
1 cup hot milk
3 teaspoons peppermint syrup or extract
6 teaspoons chocolate syrup
Ground cinnamon, for topping

Instructions:

1. Brew coffee in Takeya pitcher (page 22).
2. Heat the milk in a small saucepan on medium heat. Fold in the peppermint and chocolate syrup. Whisk until the milk becomes frothy.
3. Divide the coffee into 4 mugs and pour in the milk mixture on top of each.
4. Spoon some of the milk foam on top. Garnish with cinnamon.

10

Chocolate & Caramel Coffees

Amaretto and Chocolate Coffee

*Servings: 4 | Prep Time: 5 minutes |
Cook Time: 12 - 24 hours*

Whip up a taste of Italy and grab one complex, rich coffee drink for dessert. Amaretto mixed with chocolate and robust coffee is sure to impress any dinner guest or curl up with one as a relaxing nightcap.

Ingredients:
14-16 tablespoons coffee, coarsely ground
1 quart cold, filtered water
4 ounces Italian almond liqueur, like Amaretto
4 ounces crème de cacao
4 parts boiling water
Whipped cream (optional)

Instructions:
1. Brew coffee in Takeya pitcher (page 22).
2. Divide the coffee between 4 mugs. Add 1-part boiling water and 1-ounce each of Italian almond liqueur and crème de cacao to each mug. Top with whipped cream.

Black Magic Chocolate Coffee

*Servings: 4 | Prep Time: 5 minutes |
Cook Time: 12 - 24 hours*

This low-calorie treat is perfect for the coffee lover who enjoys a cuppa after dinner. Chocolate hazelnut meets dark rum for one sincerely rich explosion of sweet and savory dessert coffee.

Ingredients:

14-16 tablespoons coffee, coarsely ground
1 quart cold, filtered water
2 teaspoons chocolate extract
2 teaspoons hazelnut extract
2 teaspoons dark rum
1 teaspoon sugar or sugar substitute
4 tablespoon half and half
4 parts boiling water
Natural whipped cream, like Truwhip (optional topping)

Instructions:

1. Add water to Takeya pitcher and spoon coffee, chocolate extract, hazelnut extract, rum, and sugar into the infuser.
2. Brew coffee in Takeya pitcher (page 22).
3. Divide coffee between four mugs and top with 1 part boiling water per mug.
4. Add 1 tablespoon of half and half to each mug. Stir and serve with a dollop of whipped cream.

Brown Sugar Caramel Latte

*Servings: 4 | Prep Time: 10 minutes |
Cook Time: 24 hours*

Want a perfectly balanced cup of simply sweet robust coffee? Brew up a Brown Sugar Caramel Latte to quench your sweet tooth. Serve it up at a dinner party as dessert to cap off a brilliant evening.

Ingredients:

14-16 tablespoons coffee, coarsely ground
1 quart cold, filtered water
4 tablespoons brown sugar
1/2 cup half and half
4 teaspoons caramel sauce
4 parts boiling water

Instructions:

1. Brew coffee in Takeya pitcher (page 22).
2. Get the half and half out of the refrigerator, set it aside and bring it to room temperature.
3. Divide the coffee between 4 mugs; top each with one part boiling water.
4. Stir 1 tablespoon brown sugar into each mug of hot coffee until it is dissolved and a little frothy.
5. Stir in 1 tablespoon of caramel sauce and enough half and half to turn the coffee slightly white.
6. Serve hot with biscotti or English biscuits. Can also be served iced for a sweet afternoon treat.

Caramel Macchiato

*Servings: 4 | Prep Time: 20 minutes |
Cook Time: 24 hours*

Use your Takeya Cold Brew Coffee Maker to whip up tantalizing coffeehouse style drinks right in the comfort of your own kitchen. The Carmel Macchiato is just the thing to add robust, sweet coffee to your day.

Ingredients:
14-16 tablespoons "natural processed" dark roast coffee, coarsely ground
1 quart cold, filtered water
2 cups ultra-filtered milk, like Fair Life
4 tablespoons caramel syrup
4 cups ice
Whipped cream (optional)

Instructions:
1. Brew coffee in Takeya pitcher (page 22).
2. In a blender, combine the coffee, milk, caramel syrup, and ice. Pulse until well-blended.
3. Serve immediately with whipped cream.
4. For a hot version, simply swap the ice for 4 parts boiling water and combine ingredients in four coffee mugs.

Caramel Macchiato with Homemade Vanilla Syrup

*Servings: 4 | Prep Time: 15 minutes |
Cook Time: 12 - 24 hours*

Turn your kitchen into your favorite coffee house when you turn cold brew coffee into a delicious caramel macchiato. Whip them up for Sunday brunch and serve these delicious drinks with waffles or breakfast tacos.

Ingredients:

14-16 tablespoons coffee, coarsely ground
1 quart cold, filtered water
4 tablespoons vanilla syrup
2 cups frothed milk
4 tablespoons caramel sauce
Whipped cream

For the Vanilla syrup:

2 cups warm water
2 cups sugar
2 teaspoons vanilla extract

Instructions:

1. Brew coffee in Takeya pitcher (page 22).
2. For vanilla syrup, combine the 2 cups of warm water with the sugar in a small sauce pan.
3. Heat on medium low heat; continuously stir until all of the sugar is dissolved. Remove from heat and add the vanilla extract.

4. Divide the coffee into four mugs and add vanilla syrup to each mug.
5. Pour milk into a microwave safe dish. Heat in a microwave on high for 30 seconds to 1 minute, or until steam begins to rise and the milk is frothed.
6. Divide milk evenly between each mug and top with whipped cream.
7. Drizzle one tablespoon of the caramel sauce over the whipped cream and serve.

Chocolate and Vanilla Latte

*Servings: 4 | Prep Time: 5 minutes |
Cook Time: 12 hours*

If you love latte, this delicious drink will knock your socks off. When rich chocolate meets silky vanilla—your taste buds meet the best of both worlds. This drink is a perfect sweet and creamy afternoon treat!

Ingredients:

14-16 tablespoons coffee, coarsely ground
1 quart cold, filtered water
4 tablespoons instant cocoa mix
4 tablespoons vanilla flavored coffee creamer
1 cinnamon sticks
2 cups hot milk

Instructions:

1. Add water to Takeya pitcher and spoon coffee into the infuser.
2. Break the cinnamon stick in half and push into infuser with the coffee and brew coffee in Takeya pitcher (page 22).
3. Evenly divide the coffee to 4 mugs.
4. Pour 1 tablespoon of cocoa mix, vanilla-flavored creamer, 1 cup of hot milk and stir for about 30 seconds a piece.

Mayan Coffee

*Servings: 4 | Prep Time: 10 minutes |
Cook Time: 12 - 24 hours*

This bold coffee gets its flavor from a combination of old world spices and extracts that blend to combine a delicious cup of coffee that packs one cool punch. Whip one up in the morning to really get up and go!

Ingredients:
14-16 tablespoons coffee, coarsely ground
1 quart cold, filtered water
2 tablespoons Mexican chocolate
4 cups hot milk
4 tablespoons sugar
1/2 teaspoon vanilla extract
1/2 teaspoon almond extract
1/2 teaspoon cinnamon
1/4 teaspoon cayenne pepper
Whipped cream (optional)

Instructions:
1. Brew coffee in Takeya pitcher (page 22).
2. Heat the milk in a small saucepan on medium heat.
3. Add the sugar, vanilla extract, almond extract, cinnamon, and cayenne pepper and heat until the milk starts to froth.
4. Divide the coffee into four mugs and pour the milk mixture into each mug.
   Top with whipped cream and serve immediately.

Viennese Coffee

*Servings: 4 | Prep Time: 5 minutes |
Cook Time: 24 hours*

An old fashioned favorite, Viennese Coffee gets its signature flavor from a combination of chocolate and crème de cacao. These decadent flavors make for one elegant and delicious cup of coffee.

Ingredients:

14-16 tablespoons coffee, coarsely ground
1 quart cold, filtered water
8 tablespoons chocolate syrup
2 tablespoons brown sugar
1/2 cup crème de cacao
1 cup heavy whipping cream

Instructions:

1. Brew coffee in Takeya pitcher (page 22).
2. Combine the coffee, chocolate syrup and sugar in a medium saucepan. Cook over low heat for about 20 minutes.
3. Fold in the heavy cream and crème de cacao, and cook for an additional 10 minutes.
4. Divide coffee into four mugs and serve immediately.

Whipped Chocolate and Vanilla Mocha

*Servings: 4 | Prep Time: 20 minutes |
Cook Time: 12 - 24 hours*

Combine the best of both worlds when vanilla meets whipped chocolate for one rich, velvety coffee drink. If you love your desserts decadent this coffee is just for you!

Ingredients:
14-16 tablespoons coffee, coarsely ground
1 quart cold, filtered water
1 cup whipped cream, like Truwhip
3 tablespoons cocoa powder
4 teaspoons white chocolate chips
1/4 cup vanilla flavored coffee creamer
4 parts boiling water
1 cup ice cubes

Instructions:
1. Brew coffee in Takeya pitcher (page 22).
2. Whisk cocoa powder into whipped cream. Cover and refrigerate until cold brew coffee is ready.
3. Divide the coffee between four mugs. Top each with one part boiling water.
4. Pour vanilla creamer and white chocolate chips into a microwave safe bowl. Heat for 30 seconds and whisk until well-blended. Divide vanilla mocha creamer between the mugs and stir well. Top each with chocolate whipped cream and serve. Alternatively, you can serve this version iced by using ice in place of the boiling water and blending all ingredients until well-blended in a blender.

11

Mocha Coffees

Caramel Cream Mocha

*Servings: 4 | Prep Time: 10 minutes |
Cook Time: 12 - 24 hours*

Want to know how to mix up the richest, most decadent mocha you've ever had? Caramel Cream Mocha is one of the most delicious drinks you'll try in this book!

Ingredients:
14-16 tablespoons coffee, coarsely ground
1 quart cold, filtered water
1/2 cup heavy whipping cream
1 tablespoon sugar
1 teaspoon vanilla extract
1/4 cup cocoa powder
2 cups half and half
1/2 cup caramel syrup
Whipped cream (optional)

Instructions:
1. Brew coffee in Takeya pitcher (page 22).
2. In a saucepan, combine the coffee, sugar, vanilla, cocoa powder, half and half, and caramel syrup. Heat on low-medium until the mixture becomes frothy and slightly thickened.
3. Remove from heat and divide into four mugs, top with whipped cream and serve immediately.

Easy Cinnamon Mocha Latte

Servings: 4 | Prep Time: 5 minutes |
Cook Time: 12 - 24 hours

Turn your kitchen into your favorite coffee corner and whip up a cafe style latte right at home. Infused with cinnamon, this chocolate sweet drink is a great way to add some spice to your morning java.

Ingredients:

14-16 tablespoons coffee, coarsely ground
1 quart cold, filtered water
4 cups milk
2 cinnamon sticks, broken in half
8 teaspoons cocoa powder

Instructions:

1. Place cinnamon sticks with ground coffee into Takeya infuser and brew coffee (page 22).
2. Heat the milk over medium heat, in a saucepan.
3. Whisk in the cocoa powder; remove from heat when the milk begins to froth.
4. Divide the coffee between four mugs.
5. Fill each mug with frothed milk mix. Stir and enjoy.

Hot Cocoa Mocha Latte

*Servings: 4 | Prep Time: 20 minutes |
Cook Time: 5 minutes*

Hot chocolate lovers will fall fast for this decadent drink filled with hot cocoa. This sweet coffee drink is saturated with dreamy chocolate and the ever so slightly flavor of almonds. If you love hot cocoa, you'll fall in love with this recipe!

Ingredients:
14-16 tablespoons coffee, coarsely ground
1 quart cold, filtered water
2 packages hot cocoa mix
1 1/3 cups almond milk
4 tablespoons chocolate syrup
4 parts boiling water
Whipped cream (optional)

Instructions:
1. Brew coffee in Takeya pitcher (page 22).
2. Divide the coffee between four mugs.
3. Pour boiling water into four mugs or glasses.
4. Stir in half a package of the hot cocoa mix into each mug.
5. Add 1/4 of the almond milk and chocolate syrup. Top with whipped cream if desired.
6. Can also be served iced for a cool and creamy treat! Just swap the boiling water for ice and serve.

Mint Mocha Latte

Servings: 4 | Prep Time: 10 minutes | Cook Time: 5 minutes

If you love the creamy, cool combination of peppermint and chocolate, you'll fall in love with this sweet latte. Whip one up to start your day for a fresh kick on your morning cup of java.

Ingredients:
14-16 tablespoons coffee, coarsely ground
1 quart cold, filtered water
2 cups frothed milk
2 tablespoons peppermint syrup
3 tablespoons chocolate syrup
Whipped cream (optional)

Instructions:
1. Brew coffee in Takeya pitcher (page 22).
2. Heat the milk in a small saucepan on low-medium heat.
3. Add the peppermint syrup and chocolate syrup. Whisk until frothed.
4. Divide the coffee into 4 mugs and top each with 1/4 of the frothed milk and stir well. Top with whipped cream.

Peanut Butter Mocha

*Servings: 4 | Prep Time: 5 minutes |
Cook Time: 12 - 24 hours*

Peanut butter lovers jump for joy! Super easy to make, this fun treat combines coffee, peanut butter and chocolate for one amazingly decadent coffee experience.

Ingredients:
14-16 tablespoons coffee, coarsely ground
1 quart cold, filtered water
2 packets hot chocolate mix
1 cup milk
4 teaspoons creamy peanut butter
1 cup vanilla ice cream

Instructions:
1. Brew coffee in Takeya pitcher (page 22). Divide the coffee between 4 mugs.
2. Warm the milk in a microwave safe bowl for 30 seconds to 1 minute, or until hot.
3. Whisk the hot chocolate mix and peanut butter into the milk.
4. Top coffee with hot peanut butter mocha mix and ice cream. Serve and enjoy!

Peppermint Mocha

*Servings: 4 | Prep Time: 5 minutes |
Cook Time: 12 - 24 hours*

Another holiday treat, the peppermint mocha is an energizing treat on a cold winter's day. Infused with delicious peppermint, enjoy this delicious drink both hot or cold for a sweet morning boost.

Ingredients:

14-16 tablespoons coffee, coarsely ground
1 quart cold, filtered water
2 package hot cocoa mix
2 cups frothed milk
4 teaspoons peppermint syrup or crème de menthe
Whipped cream (optional)

Instructions:

1. Brew coffee in Takeya pitcher (page 22).
2. Pour milk into a microwave safe dish.
3. Heat in a microwave on high for 30 seconds to 1 minute, or until steam begins to rise on the milk.
4. Whisk hot cocoa into frothed milk.
5. Divide the coffee into two mugs and add one 1/2 cup of cocoa milk and 1 teaspoon peppermint syrup to coffee.
6. Top with whipped cream if desired and served.
7. Swap the peppermint syrup for crème de menthe, add some ice and turn this sweet treat into a holiday cocktail.

Salted Caramel Mocha Frappuccino

*Servings: 4 | Prep Time: 10 minutes |
Cook Time: 12 - 24 hours*

Turn your favorite sweets into one sweet, salty drink with this delicious frappuccino. Cool and creamy this drink is perfect on a hot day or fall afternoon!

Ingredients:
14-16 tablespoons coffee, coarsely ground
1 quart cold, filtered water
4 tablespoons caramel syrup
2 teaspoon sea salt
3 tablespoons chocolate syrup
4 cups ice cubes
Whipped cream (optional)

Instructions:
1. Brew coffee in Takeya pitcher (page 22).
2. Add the ice cubes, caramel syrup, sea salt, chocolate syrup, and coffee to a blender. Blend well.
3. Divide into 4 glasses. Top with whipped cream if desired.

Simple Cafe Mocha

*Servings: 4 | Prep Time: 10 minutes |
Cook Time: 12 - 24 hours*

If you love coffeehouse mochas this recipe is for you! Rich, comforting, and simple to make, this take on the classic mocha coffee drink can be made in minutes thanks to your Takeya Cold Brew Coffee Maker.

Ingredients:
14-16 tablespoons coffee, coarsely ground
1 quart cold, filtered water
4 tablespoons cocoa powder
4 teaspoons sugar or sugar substitute
4 cups milk
2 teaspoons vanilla extract

Instructions:
1. Brew coffee in Takeya pitcher (page 22).
2. Combine the milk, cocoa powder, and sugar in a small sauce pan over medium heat. Stir until sugar is completely dissolved and the milk begins to froth.
3. Divide the coffee into four mugs and top with the mocha mixture. Stir well and serve hot.

12

Fruity and Spiced Coffees

Banana Coconut Coffee Frappe

*Servings: 4 | Prep Time: 30 minutes |
Cook Time: 12 - 24 hours*

Mix up a Hawaiian influenced coffee drink that combines the earthy flavor of toasted coconut with banana and cold brewed coffee for a refreshing and sweet treat that is great any time of day.

Ingredients:
14-16 tablespoons coffee, coarsely ground
1 quart cold, filtered water
2 bananas, frozen and sliced
2 cups coconut milk
1 teaspoon vanilla extract
1 cup ice cubes

Instructions:
1. Brew coffee in Takeya pitcher (page 22).
2. Combine the coffee, banana, coconut milk, vanilla, and ice cubes in a blender.
3. Blend until smooth.
4. Pour into four tall glasses and serve with a straw.

Berry Mocha

*Servings: 4 | Prep Time: 5 minutes |
Cook Time: 12 - 24 hours*

Impress your after dinner guests with a refreshing coffee drink that is sure to liven up any night in. Bright sweet berries turn robust coffee and decadent chocolate into one tantalizing cup of joe.

Ingredients:
14-16 tablespoons coffee, coarsely ground
1 quart cold, filtered water
2 cups hot milk
4 package hot cocoa mix
2 tablespoons strawberry syrup
2 tablespoons raspberry syrup
2 tablespoons blueberry syrup
Whipped cream, for topping

Instructions:
1. Brew coffee in Takeya pitcher (page 22).
2. Divide the coffee between four mugs.
3. Heat the milk in a small saucepan on medium heat.
4. Add the hot cocoa powder and berry syrups; whisk until well-blended.
5. Heat berry mixture until the milk becomes frothy.
6. Pour the milk mixture evenly into all four mugs, stir, and top with whipped cream to serve.

Blueberry White Chocolate Latte

*Servings: 4 | Prep Time: 5 minutes |
Cook Time: 12 - 24 hours*

This delicious coffee drink combines subtle hints of fruit and white chocolate to add something different to your usual cup of java. The sweet flavors in this drink really shine with Takeya's cold brew coffee.

Ingredients:

14-16 tablespoons coffee, coarsely ground
1 quart cold, filtered water
2 cups hot milk
4 tablespoons white chocolate sauce
4 tablespoons blueberry syrup
Whipped cream, for topping
Ground cinnamon, for topping

Instructions:

1. Brew coffee in Takeya pitcher (page 22).
2. Heat the milk in a small saucepan on medium heat. Fold in the white chocolate sauce and blueberry syrup. Stir and continue to heat until the milk begins to froth.
3. Divide the cold brew between 4 mugs and pour 1/2 of the milk into each one.
4. Top with whipped cream and a dash of ground cinnamon to garnish.

Chocolate-Cherry Frappe

*Servings: 4 | Prep Time: 10 minutes |
Cook Time: 12 - 24 hours*

Full of rich coffee and chocolate, with a bright burst of cherry, this frappe is just the thing to quench your sweet tooth. Perfect for and after dinner treat or after school snack.

Ingredients:
14-16 tablespoons coffee, coarsely ground
1 quart cold, filtered water
1/4 cup coconut or almond milk
1 cup vanilla yogurt
1 cup frozen cherries
2 teaspoon cocoa powder
1 tablespoon sugar or sugar substitute
3 cups ice cubes
Whipped cream (optional)

Instructions:
1. Brew coffee in Takeya pitcher (page 22).
2. Divide the coffee between four mugs.
3. Pour the coffee, ice, cherries, cocoa powder, milk, yogurt and sugar into a blender.
4. Blend until the cherries have broken down completely and there are no chunks.
5. Divide into four chilled glasses and top with whipped cream if desired.

Coconut Oil Coffee

*Servings: 4 | Prep Time: 5 minutes |
Cook Time: 12 - 24 hours*

For sustained energy and rich flavor this strong cup of coffee can't be beat. If you love your morning cuppa, you might just fall in love with the subtle hint of coconut in this robust cold brew.

Ingredients:

14-16 tablespoons coffee, coarsely ground
1 quart cold, filtered water
4 parts boiling water
4 tablespoons coconut oil
4 tablespoons unsalted butter
4 tablespoons half and half (optional)

Instructions:

1. Brew coffee in Takeya pitcher (page 22).
2. Divide the coffee between four mugs.
3. Top each with one 1-part boiling water.
4. Stir in 1 teaspoon of coconut oil and butter to each mug until dissolved and frothy.
5. For a slightly less intense flavor try adding a tablespoon of half and half to each mug, and serve.

Honey Coffee

*Servings: 4 | Prep Time: 5 minutes |
Cook Time: 12 - 24 hours*

Brew up one deliciously rich cup of coffee with a depth of flavor that tantalizes the taste buds. This amazing coffee combines different spices with sweet honey— for one amazing cuppa.

Ingredients:
14-16 tablespoons coffee, coarsely ground
1 quart cold, filtered water
1 cup milk
1/4 cup honey
1/2 teaspoon ground cinnamon
1/4 teaspoon ground nutmeg
1/2 teaspoon vanilla extract

Instructions:
1. Brew coffee in Takeya pitcher (page 22).
2. In a saucepan, combine the coffee, spices, milk, and honey and heat on medium until well blended. Remove from the heat and add the vanilla.
3. Divide into two mugs and serve immediately.

Raspberry Frappe

*Servings: 4 | Prep Time: 20 minutes |
Cook Time: 12 - 24 hours*

Whip up a fruit infused treat to give your coffee a bright boost. Whether you're serving Raspberry Frappes for dessert or as a mid-morning snack, they are also a fun way to start the day.

Ingredients:
14-16 tablespoons coffee, coarsely ground
1 quart cold, filtered water
1 cup half and half or whole milk
1/4 cup raspberry syrup
3 cups coffee ice cream
2 cups ice cubes
Whipped cream (optional)

Instructions:
1. Brew coffee in Takeya pitcher (page 22).
2. Pour the coffee, milk, raspberry syrup, ice cream, and ice into a blender and blend until roughly mixed.
3. Divide evenly into four tall chilled glasses and top with whipped cream, if desired.

Spiked Cherry Cola Cold Brew

*Servings: 4 | Prep Time: 25 minutes |
Cook Time: 12 - 24 hours*

Whip up one unusually tantalizing cocktail that combines lots of sweet flavors that add up to one well-balanced cold brew treat. Serve this one up on a hot summer day to chill out and cool down.

Ingredients:
14-16 tablespoons coffee, coarsely ground
1 quart cold, filtered water
2 (12-ounce) cans cherry cola
8 ounces vodka or white rum
Lime wedges, for garnish

Instructions:
1. Brew coffee in Takeya pitcher (page 22).
2. Divide coffee between the four glasses with ice.
3. Add 2 ounces vodka or rum. Top with 1/2 can of cherry cola.
4. Garnish with a lime wedge and serve with a straw.

Strawberry Iced Coffee

*Servings: 4 | Prep Time: 20 minutes |
Cook Time: 12 - 24 hours*

Whip up a taste of summer with this refreshing coffee drink. When fresh fruit meets your morning java, you get one seriously bright morning cuppa!

Ingredients:

14-16 tablespoons coffee, coarsely ground
1 quart cold, filtered water
4 teaspoons sugar or sugar substitute
2 cups cold milk
1 punnet strawberries, capped and frozen
Ice cubes
Whipped cream

Instructions:

1. Brew coffee in Takeya pitcher (page 22).
2. Combine frozen strawberries, coffee, milk and sugar in a blender. Blend until smooth.
3. Fill four glasses with ice and divide the strawberry coffee between the 4 glasses. Top with whipped cream.

13

Iced Coffees

Blended Iced Espresso

*Servings: 4 | Prep Time: 20 minutes |
Cook Time: 24 - 48 hours*

Whip up one simple blended treat in no time with your Takeya Cold Brew Coffee Maker. Iced espresso is the perfect pick me up, afternoon treat!

Ingredients:
14-16 tablespoons "natural processed" dark roast coffee, coarsely ground
1 quart cold, filtered water
2 cups cold ultra-filtered milk, like Fair Life
3 teaspoons sugar or sugar substitute
4 cups ice
Whipped cream (optional)

Instructions:
1. Brew coffee in Takeya pitcher (page 22).
2. Combine the espresso coffee, milk, sugar, and ice in a blender. Blend until smooth.
3. Divide the iced espresso between four glasses.
4. Top with whipped cream, if desired, to serve.

Caribbean Spiced Coffee Soda

*Servings: 4 | Prep Time: 20 minutes |
Cook Time: 12 - 24 hours*

This island inspired drink is part coffee, part cocktail, part soda—and 100% delicious! Surprisingly easy to make, spice up your cold brew life with a taste of the Caribbean.

Ingredients:
14-16 tablespoons coffee, coarsely ground
1 quart cold, filtered water
4 ounces Kahlua
4 ounces spiced rum
1 (12-ounce) bottle or can of cola
1/2 cup half and half

Instructions:
1. Brew coffee in Takeya pitcher (page 22).
2. In a pitcher, combine the coffee, Kahlua, rum, cola, and half and half.
3. Stir until well-blended.
4. Fill 4 glasses with ice and pour in the coffee mixture.

Chocolate-Cinnamon Iced Cappuccino

*Servings: 4 | Prep Time: 10 minutes |
Cook Time: 12 - 24 hours*

Combine the rich flavors of chocolate and cinnamon to create a rich dessert coffee that is complex and satisfying. Add a little ice and you've got one sincerely decadent iced coffee for a killer anytime treat.

Ingredients:

14-16 tablespoons coffee, coarsely ground
1 quart cold, filtered water
1 cinnamon stick, broken in half
1/2 cup sweetened condensed milk
6 tablespoons chocolate syrup
1/2 teaspoon vanilla extract
1 cup ice cubes
Whipped cream (optional)

Instructions:

1. Add water to the Takeya pitcher and spoon coffee into the infuser.
2. Push cinnamon sticks into the coffee.
3. Brew coffee in Takeya pitcher (page 22).
4. Combine the coffee, condensed milk, chocolate syrup, vanilla extract, and ice cubes in a blender. Blend until smooth.
5. Top with whipped cream and serve.

Coconut Mocha Iced Coffee

*Servings: 4 | Prep Time: 5 minutes |
Cook Time: 12 - 24 hours*

Give your taste buds something to celebrate with the soothing, naturally sweet taste of coconut. Paired with delicious chocolate, this drink is simply to do die for!

Ingredients:
14-16 tablespoons coffee, coarsely ground
1 quart cold, filtered water
2 cups coconut milk
8 tablespoons chocolate syrup
4 teaspoons vanilla extract
4 teaspoons sugar or sugar substitute
Ice

Instructions:
1. Brew coffee in Takeya pitcher (page 22).
2. Pour the coffee, coconut milk, chocolate syrup, vanilla, and sugar into a blender. Blend until smooth.
3. Pour over ice and serve with a straw.

Coffee Ice Cubes

*Servings: 4 | Prep Time: 5 minutes |
Cook Time: 12 - 24 hours*

If you're looking for the best way to keep your iced coffee drinks for becoming weak and watery this is the perfect solution.

Ingredients:
14-16 tablespoons coffee, coarsely ground
1 quart cold, filtered water
1/2 cup cold milk (optional)

Instructions:
1. Brew coffee in Takeya pitcher (page 22).
2. Dilute the coffee with cold milk for creamy coffee ice cubes.
3. Pour the coffee or coffee with milk into two ice cube trays and place in the freezer for up to 4 hours or until solid.
4. Use in your favorite Takeya Cold Brew Coffee recipe for an extra kick of joe!

Cold Brewed Horchata Coffee

*Servings: 4 | Prep Time: 8 hours |
Cook Time: 10 minutes*

This recipe shows you how to combine espresso with horchata to make a creamy spiced Mexican inspired drink. You'll also learn how to make delicious horchata from scratch, too!

Ingredients:
14-16 tablespoons coffee, coarsely ground
1 quart cold, filtered water

For the Horchata:
8 tablespoons rice
1 cup unsalted raw almonds
1 teaspoon ground cinnamon
6 cups warm water
1 cup sugar
1 teaspoon vanilla extract, preferably Mexican vanilla

Instructions:
1. Brew coffee in Takeya pitcher.
2. Place the rice in a blender and blend well until the rice is powdered. In a large bowl, combine the rice, almonds, cinnamon, and water. Let stand about seven and a half hours.
3. Pour the mixture into a blender and blend until smooth. Strain several times, until there are no solids in the horchata. Pour the horchata into a pitcher and add the sugar and vanilla stirring until the sugar dissolves.
4. Fill four glasses with ice and add the coffee. Pour some horchata into each glass, stir and serve with a straw.

Cold Brewed Iced Mocha

*Servings: 4 | Prep Time: 20 minutes |
Cook Time: 12 - 48 hours*

Give your coffee one sincerely sweet twist with a touch of chocolate. If you love coffee house mocha's and iced coffee, you will fall in love with this refreshing, dreamy treat. The best part—you can make this drink sugar-free!

Ingredients:

14-16 tablespoons coffee, coarsely ground
1 quart cold, filtered water
4 cups cold ultra-filtered milk, like Fair Life
4 tablespoons chocolate syrup or sugar-free
4 teaspoons sugar or sugar-substitute
Ice

Instructions:

1. Brew coffee in Takeya pitcher (page 22).
2. Store longer for stronger coffee. Add ice and coffee to four glasses. Add one cup of the milk, and 1 tablespoon each of the chocolate syrup and sugar to each glass.
3. Stir and enjoy.

Cold Brewed Vanilla Caramel Coffee

*Servings: 4 | Prep Time: 5 minutes |
Cook Time: 12 - 24 hours*

The rich taste of cold brewed coffee really brings out the true luxurious taste of caramel when it meets creamy vanilla. A great dessert treat or just a fun way of serving coffee on a warm day, you'll fall in love with Cold Brewed Vanilla Caramel Coffee.

Ingredients:
14-16 tablespoons coffee, coarsely ground
1 quart cold, filtered water
3 cups cold milk
2 teaspoons pure vanilla extract
1/4 cup caramel ice cream topping
Crushed ice
Whipped cream, optional topping

Instructions:
1. Brew coffee in Takeya pitcher (page 22).
2. Pour the coffee, milk, and caramel sauce into a blender with about 3 cups of crushed ice. Blend well and divide evenly among 4 glasses. Serve with whipped cream.

Frozen Caramel-Cinnamon Latte

*Servings: 4 | Prep Time: 20 minutes |
Cook Time: 12 - 24 hours*

Delightfully sweet coffee frappes are just the thing to spice up any coffee lover's day. This sweet recipe combines fresh cinnamon with creamy caramel for a fun alternative to the traditional iced coffee treat.

Ingredients:

14-16 tablespoons coffee, coarsely ground
1 quart cold, filtered water
6 tablespoons caramel syrup
2 cinnamon sticks, broken in half
2 cups cold milk
1 teaspoon vanilla extract
1 cup ice cubes
1/4 teaspoon sea salt
Whipped cream (optional)

Instructions:

1. Add water to the Takeya pitcher and spoon coffee into the infuser.
2. Push cinnamon sticks into the coffee.
3. Brew coffee in Takeya pitcher (page 22).
4. Combine the coffee, milk, caramel syrup, vanilla extract, ice, and sea salt in a blender. Blend until smooth.
5. Divide into four tall glasses and top with whipped cream to serve.

Frozen Caramel Latte

*Servings: 4 | Prep Time: 2 hours |
Cook Time: 12 - 24 hours*

Perfect for summertime this frozen treat is super refreshing. Guaranteed the most flavorful cold brewed coffee ever - thanks to Takeya, to really make this drink come alive.

Ingredients:
14-16 tablespoons coffee, coarsely ground
1 quart cold, filtered water
8 tablespoons caramel syrup
3 cups cold milk
3 cups ice

Instructions:
1. Brew coffee in Takeya pitcher (page 22).
2. Pour the cold brewed coffee into 3-4 ice cube trays and place in the freezer until solid; about 2 hours.
3. Combine the frozen coffee cubes, caramel syrup, milk, and ice in a blender. Blend until smooth.
4. Divide amongst four glasses and serve with a straw!

Hazelnut Mocha Smoothie

*Servings: | Prep Time: 10 minutes |
Cook Time: 12 - 24 hours*

Give your mornings a nutty kick with the rich nutty flavor of Nutella. Also a great way to combine coffee and dessert into one easy dish, you'll love this drink.

Ingredients:

14-16 tablespoons coffee, coarsely ground
1 quart cold, filtered water
1 1/2 cups cold milk
1/2 cup Nutella
2 cups ice
4 cups vanilla or coffee ice cream
Whipped cream (optional)

Instructions:

1. Brew coffee in Takeya pitcher (page 22).
2. Pour the coffee over the ice to cool.
3. Pour the coffee, ice, milk, Nutella, and vanilla ice cream into a blender. Blend until smooth and divide into 4 tall, chilled glasses. Top with whipped cream and serve with straw.

Honey Cinnamon Iced Coffee

*Servings: Prep Time: 25 minutes |
Cook Time: 12 - 24 hours*

Brew up one sweet and spicy iced coffee that uses honey for an earthier sweetness than sugar. That natural coffee flavor really shines through in this robust drink!

Ingredients:
14-16 tablespoons coffee, coarsely ground
1 quart cold, filtered water
4 tablespoons honey
2 cinnamon sticks
2 cups cold milk
Ice

Instructions:
1. Add water to the Takeya pitcher and spoon coffee into the infuser.
2. Push cinnamon sticks into the coffee. Brew coffee in Takeya pitcher (page 22).
3. Combine the coffee, honey, and milk in a blender. Blend until smooth.
4. Fill 4 glasses with ice and pour in the coffee mixture. Serve with straw.

Iced Coconut Latte

*Servings: 4 | Prep Time: 20 minutes |
Cook Time: 12 - 24 hours*

Blend up one island inspired drink for one bold afternoon pick me up. Sweetness of real coconut milk with the rich, bold flavor of Takeya coffee is sure to help you escape. This recipe shows you how to serve it cold, but it can also be made as a hot latte as well.

Ingredients:

14-16 tablespoons coffee, coarsely ground
1 quart cold, filtered water
8 tablespoons coconut milk
8 tablespoons caramel syrup
2 cups cold milk
1 cup ice cubes

Instructions:

1. Brew coffee in Takeya pitcher (page 22).
2. Add the coconut milk and caramel syrup to the cold milk and stir until well-blended.
3. Fill four glasses with ice and divide the coffee between the glasses. Top each with 1/4 coconut milk mixture. Stir well and serve with a straw.

Old Fashioned Coffee Soda

*Servings: 4 | Prep Time: 25 minutes |
Cook Time: 48 hours*

A traditional recipe with double the strength cold brewed coffee, this drink is sure to add a spark to your morning routine. This fizzy coffee soda is also delicious with your favorite syrup added in for a little flavor.

Ingredients:
14-16 tablespoons "natural processed" dark roast coffee, coarsely ground
1 quart cold, filtered water
4 cups club soda
4 tablespoons half and half
Ice cubes

Instructions:
1. Brew coffee in Takeya pitcher (page 22).
2. Fill four glasses with ice and divide the coffee between them. Add 1 tablespoon of the half and half to teach glass.
3. Top each with 1 cup of club soda, stir and enjoy!

Simple Coffee Frappe

*Servings: 4 | Prep Time: 5 minutes |
Cook Time: 12 - 24 hours*

Curl up with a sweet, simple treat that is so easy to make - you'll fall in love with this yummy frappe. Perfect after a morning workout or to put a spring in your afternoon step.

Ingredients:
14-16 tablespoons coffee, coarsely ground
1 quart cold, filtered water
1/2 cup milk
2 cups vanilla ice cream
2 tablespoons sugar or sugar substitute
Whipped cream (optional)

Instructions:
1. Brew coffee in Takeya pitcher (page 22).
2. Pour the coffee into a blender with the milk, ice cream, and sugar. Blend until smooth.
3. Divide into four tall glasses.
4. Top with whipped cream if desired and enjoy!

Simple Cold Brewed Coffee

*Servings: 4 | Prep Time: 3 minutes |
Cook Time: 12 - 48 hours*

Super easy to make, Takeya Cold Brew is the best way to make robust coffee. Whether you love an ice cold cup or mug of hot coffee, Takeya is designed to make the world's best tasting cold brewed coffee!

Ingredients:

14-16 tablespoons coffee, coarsely ground
1 quart cold, filtered water
Half and half (optional)
Sugar or sugar substitute (optional)

Instructions:

1. Brew coffee in Takeya pitcher (page 22).
2. Top with one part boiling water for a hot coffee, or fill a glass with ice and top ice with coffee for a cold drink.
3. Stir in your favorite creamer, sugar or sugar substitute and enjoy!

14

International Coffees

African Coffee Punch

*Servings: 10 | Prep Time: 5 minutes |
Cook Time: 12 - 24 hours*

Put a punch in your next party with this unusual and exciting cold brew coffee drink. The African inspired party punch combines tantalizing liquors and coffee to make something truly unexpected.

Ingredients:
14-16 tablespoons coffee, coarsely ground
1 quart cold, filtered water
2 cups boiling water
1 bottle brandy
1/2 bottle white rum
1 cup brown sugar
Whipped cream, for topping

Instructions:
1. Brew coffee in Takeya pitcher (page 22).
2. Pour boiling water into a large punch bowl. Fold in sugar and stir until it's completely dissolved.
3. Slowly add brandy, rum, and coffee.
4. Stir until well blended.
5. Ladle one serving into a mug and top with whipped cream, if desired.

Authentic Irish Coffee

*Servings: 4 | Prep Time: 5 minutes |
Cook Time: 12 - 24 hours*

The perfect after dinner coffee, this drink is the result of a blend of delicious and simple flavors. Serve one up as a night cap or end to a perfect evening - enjoy responsibly!

Ingredients:
14-16 tablespoons coffee, coarsely ground
1 quart cold, filtered water
4 parts boiling water
4 teaspoons brown sugar
6 ounces Irish whiskey
Heavy cream, slightly whipped

Instructions:
1. Brew coffee in Takeya pitcher (page 22).
2. Divide the coffee between 4 mugs and top with one part boiling water each.
3. Add the brown sugar. Stir until the sugar is completely dissolved.
4. Add 1 ounce of whiskey to each mug.
5. Whip the heavy cream until it is halfway to stiff whipped cream.
6. Spoon about 4 tablespoons of cream onto each mug and serve immediately.

Brazilian Coffee

*Servings: 4 | Prep Time: 5 minutes |
Cook Time: 12 - 24 hours*

Brighten up your night in with a sweet citrus zing! Coffee inspired by Brazilian culture might be just the thing to unwind with on a hot summer night or snowy day in.

Ingredients:
14-16 tablespoons coffee, coarsely ground
1 quart cold, filtered water
4 ounces brandy
4 ounces grand marnier
4 ounces cachaça or brazilian liqueur
4 parts boiling water
Whipped cream
Ground cinnamon, for sprinkling

Instructions:
1. Brew coffee in Takeya pitcher (page 22).
2. Divide the coffee between 4 mugs. Top each coffee with one part boiling water and 1-ounce of the brandy, Grand Marnier, Brazilian liqueur, to each mug. Stir well.
3. Top each mug with a dollop of whipped cream and sprinkle with cinnamon.

Brazilian Coffee Soda

*Servings: 4 | Prep Time: 20 minutes |
Cook Time: 12 - 24 hours*

Brew up one fun, fizzy way to sweeten and enjoy the robust flavor of Takeya cold brew coffee. Infused with rich chocolate to add another layer of flavor, and laced with sugar cane liquor taste of Brazil—and you've got one seriously sweet coffee drink!

Ingredients:
14-16 tablespoons "natural processed" dark roast coffee, coarsely ground
1 quart cold, filtered water
1 (12-ounce) can cola, like coca cola or pepsi
4 tablespoons chocolate sauce
2 cups vanilla ice cream
4 ounces cachaça or brazilian liquor

Instructions:
1. Brew coffee in Takeya pitcher (page 22).
2. Combine the coffee, cola, liquor and chocolate sauce in a large pitcher.
3. Scoop 1/4 of the ice cream into four glasses and top with 1/4 of the coffee mixture in. Serve immediately.

Cuban Iced Coffee

*Servings: 4 | Prep Time: 25 minutes |
Cook Time: 12 - 24 hours*

This light refreshing coffee cocktail combines robust coffee flavor with a taste of the islands. A perfect beverage for unwinding after a long day. It's like a mini vacation in a cup—all courtesy of Takeya.

Ingredients:
14-16 tablespoons coffee, coarsely ground
1 quart cold, filtered water
1 tablespoon sugar
4 ounces white rum
2 cups cold milk
Mint leaves
Ice cubes

Instructions:
1. Brew coffee in Takeya pitcher (page 22).
2. In a tall glass, muddle the mint leaves with the sugar.
3. Fill each glass with ice. Add the rum and stir. Divide the coffee amongst the four glasses.
4. Stir half of the milk into each glass and garnish with a mint leaf.

Dublin Iced Coffee

*Servings: 4 | Prep Time: 25 minutes |
Cook Time: 12 - 24 hours*

This rich and thick coffee cocktail is well rounded and robust thanks to a wide variety of flavors. This isn't your traditional Irish coffee, so drink responsibly.

Ingredients:
14-16 tablespoons coffee, coarsely ground
1 quart cold, filtered water
8 ounces dark beer, preferably Guinness
4 ounces Irish whiskey
1 tablespoon sugar
4 tablespoons heavy cream
Ice

Instructions:
1. Brew coffee in Takeya pitcher (page 22).
2. In a separate pitcher stir together the coffee, beer, whiskey and sugar.
3. Fill 4 glasses with ice. Top ice with 1-part of coffee mix.
4. Add 1 tablespoon of cream to each glass and gently stir.

Guatemalan Hop

*Servings: 4 | Prep Time: 5 minutes |
Cook Time: 12 - 24 hours*

Brew up one tasty Central American treat and add a little hop to your step. Liqueur and the robust flavor of Takeya Cold Brew turn Guatemalan coffee into a truly unique after dinner drink.

Ingredients:
14-16 tablespoons Guatemalan coffee, coarsely ground
1 quart cold, filtered water
4 ounces rum
4 ounces crème de cacao
4 ounce half and half
4 parts boiling water
Whipped cream (optional)

Instructions:
1. Brew coffee in Takeya pitcher (page 22).
2. Divide the coffee between 4 mugs. Add 1-ounce rum and crème de cacao to each mug. Top with one part boiling water each and 1-ounce half and half.
3. Stir well and serve topped with whipped cream, if desired.

Irish Cappuccino

*Servings: 4 | Prep Time: 5 minutes |
Cook Time: 12 -24 hours*

Combine the flavors of two old-fashioned coffee favorites for one relaxing cup of joe. When Irish meets Italian, you'll get one killer taste explosion. Brew up some Irish Cappuccinos as the perfect after dinner treat or way to warm up on a cold winter's night.

Ingredients:

14-16 tablespoons "natural processed" dark roast coffee, coarsely ground
1 quart cold, filtered water
4 parts boiling water
8 ounces heavy cream
4 ounces Irish whisky
4 ounces Amaretto
4 teaspoons sugar or sugar substitute
Ground cinnamon to garnish

Instructions:
1. Brew coffee in Takeya pitcher (page 22).
2. Divide the coffee between 4 mugs and top each with one part boiling water.
3. Dissolve 1 teaspoon sugar into each mug and add 1-ounce heavy cream to each drink.
4. Slowly pour in one ounce of Irish whisky and Amaretto to each mug.
5. Sprinkle on a dash of cinnamon and serve immediately.

Mexican Espresso

Servings: 4 | Prep Time: 5 minutes |
Cook Time: 24 - 48 hours

Give your morning coffee a robust twist on when you whip up a not so traditional Mexican coffee. If you like dark coffee you'll adore this strong, smooth creamy, never bitter, cup of java.

Ingredients:
14-16 tablespoons "natural processed" dark roast coffee, coarsely ground
1 quart cold, filtered water
4 parts boiling water
4 ounces coffee liqueur, like Kahlua
4 teaspoons sugar or sugar substitute
Whipped cream (optional)

Instructions:
1. Brew coffee in Takeya pitcher (page 22).
2. Divide the coffee between 4 mugs.
3. Top each with one part boiling water.
   Add the coffee liqueur and sugar to the coffee.
4. Top with whipped cream to serve.

Spicy Thai Iced Coffee

Servings: 4 | Prep Time: 5 minutes | Cook Time: 12 hours

Add the taste of Asia to your morning coffee with Spicy Thai Iced Coffee. This sweet and sultry spiced treat will add a killer kick to your morning get up and go.

Ingredients:

14-16 tablespoons coffee, coarsely ground
1 quart cold, filtered water
1/2 teaspoon ground coriander
2 cardamom pods
1/2 teaspoon ground cinnamon
4 tablespoons sweetened condensed milk
4 tablespoon half and half
3 cups of cold, filtered water
Ice

Instructions:

1. Add water to Takeya pitcher.
2. Break open the cardamom pods using the handle of a knife.
3. Spoon the coffee, coriander and cinnamon into the chamber into the infuser.
4. Place the cardamom pods in the infuser with coffee and spices.
5. Twist infuser into the lid. Place infuser in the pitcher. Twist and seal lid into the pitcher airtight.
6. Shake well and place in the refrigerator for 12 hours; refrigerate longer for stronger coffee.

7. Add ice to each glass or tumbler. Divide coffee between glasses and pour coffee over ice.
8. Add 1 tablespoon of the condensed milk and half and half to each glass; stir well and enjoy.

Thai Coffee

*Servings: 4 | Prep Time: 5 minutes |
Cook Time: 12 - 24 hours*

An exotic way to spice up your daily cup of coffee, the delicate blend of flavors in this recipe are absolutely exquisite. Enjoy Thai Coffee as an anytime treat.

Ingredients:

14-16 tablespoons coffee, coarsely ground
1 quart cold, filtered water
1 cardamom pod
2 tablespoons sweetened condensed milk

Instructions:

1. Add water to the Takeya pitcher. And poon coffee into the infuser.
2. Break open the cardamom pod with the handle of a knife. Push broken pod into the coffee.
3. Brew coffee in Takeya pitcher (page 22).
4. Divide the coffee between 4 mugs and pour one tablespoon of condensed milk into each cup.
5. Stir well and enjoy.

The World's Best Pumpkin Spice Latte

*Servings: 4 | Prep Time: 15 minutes |
Cook Time: 24 hours*

You knew you would find this insanely amazing recipe eventually... The Pumpkin Spice Latte, which has become a seasonal phenomenon that can't be ignored, is one savory sweet and dreamy treat. So here it is, the best pumpkin spice latte you've ever had!

Ingredients:
14-16 tablespoons "natural processed" dark roast coffee, coarsely ground
1 quart cold, filtered water
4 tablespoons pure pumpkin, canned
1 teaspoon allspice
1 teaspoon cinnamon
4 tablespoons brown sugar
2 teaspoons vanilla extract
2 cups half and half
4 parts boiling water
Whipped cream (optional)

Instructions:
1. Brew coffee in Takeya pitcher (page 22).
2. Combine the canned pumpkin and spices in small saucepan. Heat on medium heat; stir until well combined.
3. Whisk in the sugar and continue to mix until it has the consistency of syrup; reduce heat.
4. Stir in the vanilla extract.
5. Slowly fold in the half and half.

6. Return pumpkin mix to medium heat until half and half starts to froth; about 2-3 minutes.
7. Divide the coffee into four mugs. Top each with 1/4 of the pumpkin latte.
8. Top with whipped cream if desired and enjoy!

Traditional Turkish Coffee

*Servings: 4 | Prep Time: 5 minutes |
Cook Time: 48 hours*

A rich and robust drink, Traditional Turkish Coffee is a daily custom in Turkey and one that is very important for social gatherings. Similar to espresso, this coffee is spiced with the warm, pungent aroma of cardamom—an ancient spice fit for royals.

Ingredients:
14-16 tablespoons coffee, coarsely ground
1 quart cold, filtered water
2 cardamom pods
1/3 cup boiling water, per serving
1 teaspoon sugar, per serving (optional)

Instructions:
1. Add water to Takeya pitcher.
2. Spoon coffee into the infuser. Break the cardamom pods open by smashing each with the handle of a knife; place open pods into the infuser with coffee.
3. Brew coffee in Takeya pitcher (page 22).
4. Pour the coffee into a mug.
5. Add 1/3 cup boiling water to serve hot; this coffee should be served very strong. Add sugar if desired.
6. Stir and serve.

Vietnamese Coffee

Servings: 4 | Prep Time: 20 minutes | Cook Time: 24 hours

Enjoy this delicious street coffee right at home! Strong and sweet, traditional Vietnamese coffee is for those that love a rich drink to start the day or an indulgent finish to dinner.

Ingredients:
14-16 tablespoons coffee, coarsely ground
1 quart cold, filtered water
4 parts boiling water
8 tablespoons sweetened condensed milk
Ice

Instructions:
1. Brew coffee in Takeya pitcher (page 22).
2. Combine the coffee and boiling water in a separate pitcher.
3. Add 2 tablespoons of condensed milk to each glass.
4. Top with hot coffee.
5. Add a few cubes of ice to each and enjoy!

Warm Gingerbread Irish Coffee

Servings: 4 | Prep Time: 5 minutes | Cook Time: 12 - 24 hours

Warm things up any day of the year with this modern update to the traditional Irish coffee. Fun and tantalizing this warm drink has the feeling of Fall in every delicious sip.

Ingredients:
14-16 tablespoons coffee, coarsely ground
1 quart cold, filtered water
4 ounces irish whisky
1 cup steamed milk
2 teaspoons pumpkin spice powder
Whipped cream, for topping
Ground cinnamon, for garnish

Instructions:
1. Brew coffee in Takeya pitcher (page 22).
2. Divide the coffee between 4 mugs.
3. Pour milk and pumpkin spice into a microwave safe dish. Heat in a microwave on high for 30 seconds to 1 minute, or until steam begins to rise on the milk.
4. Add the milk and Irish whisky; stir until well-blended.
5. Top with whipped cream and dust with ground cinnamon.

15

Coffee Cocktails

Cafe Imperial

*Servings: 4 | Prep Time: 5 minutes |
Cook Time: 24 hours*

A French inspired coffee drink, this one is perfect for a chilly night in or as an afterthought to a romantic dinner. This is one seriously sophisticated coffee bursting with bright flavors and a robust coffee base.

Ingredients:
14-16 tablespoons "natural processed" dark roast coffee, coarsely ground
1 quart cold, filtered water
4 parts boiling water
4 ounces orange liqueur, like Grand Marnier
4 teaspoons sugar
Whipped cream (optional topping)

Instructions:
1. Brew coffee in Takeya pitcher (page 22).
2. Divide the coffee between 4 mugs. Top with 1 part boiling water each and stir 1 teaspoon of sugar until dissolved.
3. Slowly pour in orange liqueur. Top with a dollop of whipped cream, if desired, and serve.

Cafe Rumba

Servings: 4 | Prep Time: 10 minutes |
Cook Time: 12 - 24 hours

This island inspired coffee has hints of cinnamon and dark rum for deep rich flavors. Pour your Cafe Rumba over ice for a delicious spiked ice coffee.

Ingredients:

14-16 tablespoons coffee, coarsely ground
1 quart cold, filtered water
1 cup hot milk
2 teaspoons vanilla extract
4 tablespoons sugar
8 tablespoons dark rum
2 cinnamon sticks
1 cup heavy whipping cream

Instructions:

1. Add water to the Takeya pitcher and spoon coffee into the infuser.
2. Break the cinnamon sticks in half and push them into the coffee.
3. Brew coffee in Takeya pitcher (page 22).
4. Divide the rum equally between four glasses.
5. Whip the cream in a small mixing bowl until it starts to stiffen. Fold in the sugar and vanilla extract. When the whipped cream is stiff, spoon equal amounts into the 4 glasses.
6. Pour the coffee over the whipped cream, add 1/4 cup hot milk to each glass and serve.

Chocolate Stout Affogato

Servings: 4 | Prep Time: 5 minutes | Cook Time: 5 minutes

This Italian combination of espresso, ice cream, and dark beer is as decadent as it gets, and thanks to your Takeya Cold Brew Coffee Maker, you're sure to have the most balanced flavor possible.

Ingredients:
14-16 tablespoons "natural processed" dark roast coffee, coarsely ground
1 quart cold, filtered water
4 scoops coffee ice cream
4 ounces chocolate liqueur
2 cups stout beer, like Guinness or Duclaw

Instructions:
1. Brew coffee in Takeya pitcher (page 22).
2. Place one scoop of ice cream in four chilled glasses.
3. Top each with one-part coffee.
4. Pour in 1 ounce of chocolate liqueur to each. Top with 1 cup of beer each and gently stir.
5. Serve immediately.

Coffee Liqueur

*Servings: 24 | Prep Time: 20 minutes |
Cook Time: 12 - 24 hours*

This recipe will show you how to use your Takeya Cold Brew Coffee Maker to make a flavorful version of a traditional coffee liqueur that can be enjoyed in coffee or any number of other drinks and cocktails. Perfect for the coffee lover who likes to unwind.

Ingredients:

14-16 tablespoons coffee, coarsely ground

1 quart cold, filtered water

4 cups sugar

2 tablespoons vanilla extract

4 cups vodka

Instructions:

1. Brew coffee in Takeya pitcher (page 22).
2. In a medium saucepan, combine the coffee and sugar over medium heat and bring to a boil. Simmer for about 10 minutes and remove from heat.
3. When the mixture has cooled add the vanilla extract and vodka and stir.
4. Pour the liqueur into bottles or jars and store in a cool dark place for two weeks, then use in your favorite recipes.

Creamy Cinnamon Coffee Punch

*Servings: 12 | Prep Time: 10 minutes |
Cook Time: 24 hours*

This creamy treat is perfect for entertaining when it comes to holiday parties or family gatherings. Spice things up by adding 1/4 cup of your favorite liqueur for a punchier punch.

Ingredients:
14-16 tablespoons coffee, coarsely ground
1 quart cold, filtered water
2 cups cold filtered water, for serving
2 cinnamon sticks, broken in half
1 nutmeg, cut in half
1 (12-ounce) can sweetened condensed milk
1/2 cup sugar or 1/4 cup sugar substitute
1/2 gallon vanilla ice cream

Instructions:
1. Add 10 quarts of water to the Takeya pitcher. Spoon coffee into the infuser.
2. Push cinnamon sticks and nutmeg halves into the coffee.
3. Brew coffee in Takeya pitcher (page 22).
4. Pour the coffee into a second pitcher and dilute it with the remaining water.
5. Stir in the condensed milk and sugar.
6. Scoop the ice cream into a punch bowl.
7. Slowly pour the coffee mix over the ice cream and serve with a ladle.

Creamy Spiked Coffee

*Servings: 4 | Prep Time: 5 minutes |
Cook Time: 12 - 24 hours*

Compliment your favorite cold brew coffee with a blend of delicious liqueurs and traditional spirits. This isn't your average cup of joe, so be sure to enjoy this one responsibly.

Ingredients:
14-16 tablespoons coffee, coarsely ground
1 quart cold, filtered water
4 parts boiling water
4 ounces brandy or Irish whiskey
4 ounces Irish cream
4 ounces vanilla vodka
4 ounces cinnamon schnapps

Instructions:
1. Brew coffee in Takeya pitcher (page 22).
2. Divide the coffee between four mugs and top with one part boiling water each.
3. Add 1 ounce of the brandy, Irish cream, vodka, and schnapps to each mug; stir well and serve hot.

Spiced Coffee Cocktail

*Servings: 4 | Prep Time: 25 minutes |
Cook Time: 12 - 24 hours*

Handmade cocktails are all the rage, so why not turn your crafty cold brew into something tantalizingly amazing? This sweet recipe shows you how to combine coffee, spices, and a little booze to make an out of this world cocktail treat.

Ingredients:
14-16 tablespoons coffee, coarsely ground
1 quart cold, filtered water
1/4 teaspoon ground cumin
1/2 teaspoon ground star anise
1/2 teaspoon ground cinnamon, plus more for garnish
2 teaspoons sugar
4 tablespoons half and half
4 ounces brandy or whiskey

Instructions:
1. Add water to the Takeya pitcher and spoon coffee, cumin, star anise, and ground cinnamon into the infuser.
2. Brew coffee in Takeya pitcher (page 22).
3. Whisk together the half and half, sugar, whiskey and coffee until well-combined in a large mixing bowl.
4. Pour the cocktail into four chilled martini glasses and garnish with a dash of ground cinnamon.

Summer Espresso Gin Fizz

*Servings: 4 | Prep Time: 25 minutes |
Cook Time: 12 - 24 hours*

This refreshing summer cocktail has a hint of rich coffee to offset the sweet fruit and herbal flavors of the gin to make a nice balanced beverage. Serve this one up to add a little fun to any summer day.

Ingredients:

14-16 tablespoons "natural processed" dark roast coffee, coarsely ground
1 quart cold, filtered water
6 ounces gin
12 blackberries
4 ounces simple syrup
Ice
Cold, filtered water for diluting

Instructions:

1. Brew coffee in Takeya pitcher (page 22).
2. Divide the blackberries with the simple syrup into four tumbler glasses. Muddle the fresh fruit and syrup.
3. Add one and a half ounces of gin to each glass and stir.
4. Add two ounces of cold brew espresso to each glass and stir again.
5. Top with ice and cold water, and serve with a straw.

Sweet and Creamy Irish Coffee

*Servings: 4 | Prep Time: 5 minutes |
Cook Time: 12 - 24 hours*

Give your traditional Irish coffee a flavorful twist. This delicious coffee drink is just slightly sweeter and creamier than the traditional recipe, but still packs a punch that makes it the perfect after dinner drink or nightcap.

Ingredients:
14-16 tablespoons coffee, coarsely ground
1 quart cold, filtered water
4 parts boiling water
4 ounces Irish whiskey
2 ounces Irish cream liqueur
2 teaspoons light brown sugar
4 ounces heavy cream
Whipped cream (optional)

Instructions:
1. Brew coffee in Takeya pitcher (page 22).
2. Divide the coffee between 4 mugs. Top each with one part boiling water and dissolve a 1/2 teaspoon of brown sugar into each mug.
3. Add 1-ounce whiskey, 1/2-ounce Irish cream liqueur to each mug, and 1-ounce heavy cream each.
4. Top with whipped cream and serve immediately.

The Dude

*Servings: 4 | Prep Time: 25 minutes |
Cook Time: 12 - 24 hours*

Inspired by the titular character from the film The Big Lebowski, this coffee drink combines strong espresso with a White Russian for a whimsical way to entertain the film buffs in your life.

Ingredients:
14-16 tablespoons coffee, coarsely ground
1 quart cold, filtered water
2 cups cold milk
8 ounces Kahlua
4 ounces vodka
Ice cubes

Instructions:
1. Brew coffee in Takeya pitcher (page 22).
2. In a pitcher, combine the coffee, milk, Kahlua, and vodka. Stir until well-blended.
3. Fill four glasses with ice.
4. Divide the coffee evenly amongst the glasses and serve.

Warm Strawberry Vanilla Espresso Cocktail

*Servings: 4 | Prep Time: 10 minutes |
Cook Time: 12 - 24 hours*

A sweet espresso treat, this coffee cocktail has just a hint of vanilla to add a little depth to rich coffee and fruity strawberry. This recipe is sure to become a girls' night favorite or after work treat.

Ingredients:
14-16 tablespoons "natural processed" dark roast coffee, coarsely ground
1 quart cold, filtered water
4 parts boiling water
4 teaspoons strawberry syrup
4 ounces vanilla vodka
4 ounces Frangelico
1 ounce half and half
Whipped cream (optional)

Instructions:
1. Brew coffee in Takeya pitcher (page 22).
2. Divide the coffee between four mugs.
3. Top with one part boiling water and stir in 1 teaspoon of strawberry syrup to each mug.
4. Add one-ounce vodka and Frangelico.
5. Top with whipped cream and serve immediately.

16

Bonus

Desserts you Can Make with Takeya Coffee

Perhaps the reason that coffee is so often served with dessert is because they naturally go together. The rich, robust and earthy flavor of coffee just seems to pair well with a bit of sweetness. Which always makes for the perfect end to a great meal. In this section we'll take that one step further and show you how you can make desserts using Takeya coffee right in the recipe. We're going to feature two classic recipes that put the flavor of espresso right up front. First, let's talk about how to make a classic Italian dessert staple, Tiramisu. The sweetness of the mascarpone cheese is elevated with the introduction of espresso soaked lady fingers for a perfect balance of flavors.

The Perfect Takeya Tiramisu

*Servings: 8 | Prep Time: 30 minutes |
Cook Time: 10 minutes*

Ingredients:
1/4 cup Takeya Cold Brew coffee
6 egg yolks
3/4 cups sugar
2/3 cups milk
1 1/4 cups heavy cream
1/2 teaspoon vanilla extract
1 pound mascarpone cheese
2 tablespoons rum
2 packages lady finger cookies
1 tablespoon cocoa powder

Instructions:
1. Brew coffee in Takeya pitcher (page 22).
2. In a medium saucepan whisk together the egg yolks and sugar. Then add the milk and cook until the mixture reaches a boil. Remove from heat, cover and place in the refrigerator.
3. Using a mixer, beat together the heavy cream and vanilla until it becomes stiff. Then whisk in the mascarpone until thoroughly blended.
4. In another bowl stir together the espresso and rum.
5. Place the ladyfingers on a baking sheet and pour the espresso/rum mixture over them and allow to soak.
6. In a baking dish, arrange a layer of the soaked lady fingers on the bottom. Spread enough mascarpone over them to cover, and then add a layer of the whipped cream.

Then repeat these steps, starting with another layer of ladyfingers.

7. Cover the baking dish and chill in the refrigerator for at least 3 hours before serving.
8. When ready to serve, dust the top with the cocoa powder and serve immediately.

Takeya Cold Brew Coffee Cheesecake

*Servings: 10 | Prep Time: 30 minutes |
Cook Time: 60 minutes*

Cheesecake is an excellent canvas for creative flavors and this recipe will s how you how to use strong Takeya coffee to make a rich and flavorful cheesecake that is sure to wow your guests.

Ingredients:

For the filling:
1/4 cup Takeya coffee
1 tablespoon finely ground coffee
1 tablespoon water
24 ounces cream cheese
1 cup sugar
3 eggs
1/4 cup unsalted butter, melted

For the Crust:
10 ounces chocolate wafers or graham crackers
1 stick unsalted butter, melted

Instructions:
1. Brew coffee in Takeya pitcher (page 22).
2. Preheat oven to 400F.
3. In a food processor, grind the cookies and add the butter. Then press the moist cookie mixture into the bottom of a greased 9-inch pan and set aside.
4. In a bowl, mix the cream cheese until smooth and add the sugar and beat until the mixture becomes fluffy.

5. Add the eggs one at a time and then mix in the espresso, butter and ground coffee.
6. Pour the filling mixture into the crust and bake for about 40 minutes or until the top is golden brown.
7. Remove from the oven and cool on a rack for at least one hour and then place in the refrigerator for twelve hours.

Takeya Cold Brew Coffee Cheesecake

Servings: 10 | Prep Time: 30 minutes | Cook Time: 60 minutes

Cheesecake is an excellent canvas for creative flavors and this recipe will s how you how to use strong Takeya coffee to make a rich and flavorful cheesecake that is sure to wow your guests.

Ingredients:

For the filling:
1/4 cup Takeya coffee
1 tablespoon finely ground coffee
1 tablespoon water
24 ounces cream cheese
1 cup sugar
3 eggs
1/4 cup unsalted butter, melted

For the Crust:
10 ounces chocolate wafers or graham crackers
1 stick unsalted butter, melted

Instructions:
1. Brew coffee in Takeya pitcher (page 22).
2. Preheat oven to 400F.
3. In a food processor, grind the cookies and add the butter. Then press the moist cookie mixture into the bottom of a greased 9-inch pan and set aside.
4. In a bowl, mix the cream cheese until smooth and add the sugar and beat until the mixture becomes fluffy.

5. Add the eggs one at a time and then mix in the espresso, butter and ground coffee.
6. Pour the filling mixture into the crust and bake for about 40 minutes or until the top is golden brown.
7. Remove from the oven and cool on a rack for at least one hour and then place in the refrigerator for twelve hours.

Spice Up Sauces with Takeya Cold Brew Coffee

Adding some Takeya Cold Brew coffee directly to a sauce can greatly improve its depth of flavor. This traditional barbecue sauce is enhanced with the addition of a little earthy coffee flavor. It can be used on literally anything you're planning to grill or smoke.

Ingredients:

1/2 cup Takeya Cold Brew coffee
4 tablespoons minced garlic
4 tablespoons olive oil
1 cup apple cider vinegar
1/2 cup soy sauce
2 cups ketchup
2 cups honey
1 tablespoon sea salt

Instructions:

1. Brew coffee in Takeya pitcher (page 22).
2. Simply mix all the ingredients together and slather on meat before and after cooking for the most flavorful barbecue sauce you've ever had.
3. Essential Ingredients for Exciting Coffee Drinks

Extra Credit

Choose your perfect roast

Obviously the most important part of coffee is the beans and since there are so many different types of bean, choosing the right ones is important. As we discussed in an earlier chapter, the region and roast really determine the flavor so experiment with some different types and see which you prefer.

Syrups and flavors

At most upscale coffee places, you'll find a wall of different flavored syrups to enhance coffee drinks. Most of these can be purchased in a supermarket. Since you might not have room for them all, some essentials are: caramel syrup, almond, peppermint, and vanilla. With these four flavors you can create a multitude of different concoctions.

Toppings for Takeya Cold Brew Coffee

Many of the drinks we've discussed are topped with whipped cream. But is there really a difference between the whipped cream in a can and the kind you make yourself? The answer is, yes. While the canned whipped cream may be convenient, it doesn't have the firm texture of handmade whipped cream. For warm coffee drinks this is important because the thicker the cream, the better it will stand up to the hot coffee. It may take an extra few minutes, but homemade whipped cream is definitely worth it.

Homemade Whipped Cream

Ingredients:
2 tablespoons sugar
1 cup heavy cream

Instructions:
1. Place a large metal mixing bowl and whisk into the freezer to chill for 15 to 20 minutes.
2. Add sugar and heavy cream.
   Whisk vigorously until stiff peaks begin to form.
3. Top your favorite Takeya cold brew drink and store leftovers for up to three days in an airtight container in the refrigerator.

Making the Perfect Cup of Takeya Cold Brew

How to Make Your Takeya Cold Brew Drinks Diabetic Friendly

Some people may prefer a low-sugar, low-calorie or diabetic friendly drink. In that case, simply swap the sugar for sugar substitute and the syrup for one that is sugar-free. Easy as that!

Liqueurs

We've been adding liquor to coffee for a long time, and it's probably because the flavors pair so well together. To become an expert at making spiked coffees, it's a good idea to keep certain alcoholic staples on hand. Probably the most common addition to coffee would be Irish whiskey since the Irish coffee has always been a popular choice. It is also recommended to keep on hand a supply of an Irish cream like Baileys, and some flavored liqueurs such as Kahlua, Grand Marnier, and Framboise. More exotic liqueurs such as Amaretto are also good for making fun and original creations. Of course, you can try whatever flavors you like to make coffee drinks that appeal to your taste, but having these liqueurs standing by will ensure that you can whip up a batch of creative drinks any time.

Marinate Meat with Takeya Cold Brew Coffee

Coffee can be used as a preparation for meat in several different ways. We'll discuss how you can use ground coffee as a rub, or use prepared cold brew as part of a marinade to give meat a deep, earthy flavor.

Takeya Cold Brew as a rub:

This one is pretty simple but is often overlooked by grill cooks. This works best with beef, lamb, and pork, but you can try it with anything you plan to cook on the grill. When you're at the seasoning stage, add some finely ground coffee to your salt and pepper mixture and rub all over the meat. When the meat cooks, the heat from the grill will interact with the coffee to create a unique smoky flavor that will enhance the flavor of the meat.

Takeya Cold Brew as a marinade:

There are endless ways to marinate meat, but adding some Takeya Cold Brew coffee to a traditional marinade you can greatly enhance the flavor of most meats by giving it a deep complex flavor. Here's a great marinade recipe for beef, lamb, or chicken

Ingredients:

1/2 cup Takeya strong brewed coffee

3 tablespoons red wine vinegar

2 teaspoons minced garlic

1 tablespoon olive oil

1 tablespoon rosemary, preferably fresh

1 teaspoon sea salt

1 teaspoon ground pepper

1 tablespoon lemon juice

Instructions:

1. Brew coffee in Takeya pitcher (page 22).
2. In a large bowl, combine all ingredients and stir well.
3. To use, place your meat in a large plastic storage bag and pour in the marinade. Let the meat marinate for an hour or two before cooking. Don't let the meat marinate longer than three hours or it will affect the texture of the meat.